A Practical Guide to Project Management

A Practical Guide to Project Management

David A. Grootenhuis

Writers Club Press
San Jose New York Lincoln Shanghai

A Practical Guide to Project Management

Writers Club Press
an imprint of iUniverse.com, Inc.

For information address:
iUniverse.com, Inc.
5220 S 16th, Ste. 200
Lincoln, NE 68512
www.iuniverse.com

ISBN: 0-595-18521-5

Printed in the United States of America

Contents

Introduction

Why are there project managers?

Project Management as a profession grew out of the increasing speed of change in the business and industrial environments. Project management as a responsibility has existed as long as organizations have experience planned change. A *project* is an initiative within an organization designed to accomplish a specific goal. Projects have clear start dates and end dates and usually result in some change in the environment.

For many years, the area managers coordinated projects in addition to their other responsibilities. This succeeded if the manager could add the project to his or her regular workload and if the manager had the necessary skills to effectively manage projects. As the pace of change increased, managers were drawn away from their primary responsibilities more often. In addition, while most managers were very knowledgeable in the areas they manage, they may not have the project management skills to facilitate a large project. The most successful manager of engineering may lack the training and attributes necessary to manage projects. Also, a talented engineering manager should be managing engineering, not projects. Project managers benefit the business in two ways: they have the skills and training to effectively manage initiatives and they free managers and line personnel to apply their expertise to their primary responsibilities.

In many organizations, line managers are still responsible for managing projects. In these cases it is crucial that they be well versed in the techniques of project management.

Project management is a process. Project managers facilitate a team through a series of steps that bring them to decisions, plans and the completion of the initiative. Project managers document goals and actions to be taken, monitor progress, identify and assign issues, produce reports, plan and facilitate meetings and coordinate other activities that help the team achieve their goals.

Project managers are not required to have first hand knowledge of the subject of the project. The project team is made up of subject matter experts. By claiming ignorance, the project manager does not threaten the knowledge level of the team members. Team members must explain concepts and issues at a very basic level, which in turn prompts them to look at concepts and issues in basic terms. This often promotes new approaches to problems, issues and projects.

The job of the team members is to bring their expertise to the group and provide the information and abilities necessary to complete the project. The project manager's job is to orchestrate the efforts of the team members, leveraging their knowledge to complete the task at hand. The project manager must ask the key questions that prompt the group to take an objective view of their situation and think "out of the box". Once again, the project manager's expertise is in the *process*, not necessarily the *subject* of the project. The process can be applied to any situation with little modification. Project managers also bring an objective view of situations, unclouded by pre-conceived notions or routine practices.

Project management brings process expertise, organizational abilities and an objective point of view. All of these combine to allow the project manager to guide the group through the initiative at hand, ensuring that proper level of planning and forethought is engaged and providing a more detailed level of reporting to upper management. The project manager also ensures economy of effort, making sure that the team members are focused on the areas that are necessary to the success of the project and eliminating their involvement in non-crucial items.

The goal of the project manager is *Closure*. As issues are identified, they are brought to resolution and closed, project documents are developed, tasks in the project plan are completed. In all cases the project manager is focused on bringing the group to agreement and moving to the next item.

Project managers must possess a unique combination of characteristics. They must be comfortable leading group discussions, preparing detailed documents, facilitating groups to a conclusion, resolving conflicts and evaluating the relationships between the steps in a process. They must influence individuals over which they have no official authority or may, in fact, be subordinate to.

A key to successful project management is to lead by example. Those responsible for managing an initiative must complete their deliverables on schedule. A project manager that does not deliver cannot expect team members to.

Through the use of project management techniques and a refined project management process, organizations can complete initiatives on time, on budget and achieve the desired results.

CHAPTER ONE

The Project Process

The Project Process

The project management process is a series of steps designed to bring an initiative to its successful conclusion. No matter how large or small the initiative, all projects can be broken into defined steps. The main difference between large and small projects is the complexity of the planning and documentation and the length of time required to complete each phase. The basic phases are:

- Concept
- Budgeting
- Approach
- Scope
- Requirements
- Design
- Build
- Implement
- Review/Signoff

The order of the steps varies with the situation. Projects occasionally slip back and forth between adjacent steps. The "Budgeting", "Approach" and "Scope" phases are dependent upon each other and projects may revisit these steps several times before they are finalized. In some cases the

1

budget is established prior to the initiation of the project and the scope and approach will be established within the limits of the budget.

Large projects may be in several stages at the same time. For example, facilities may be acquired before the final design details are complete. (As long as the requirements of the facilities have been defined)

In the case of building a home, construction (The "Build" phase) may begin before the final aspects of the design are complete. Or, the residents of the home may move in (the "Implementation" phase) before the final aspects of construction are complete.

There are three documents that contain the details of the Project Process. The Project Charter contains the Concept, Budgeting, Approach and Scope. The Project Plan outlines the Requirements, Design, Build and Implements phases. The Signoff Document covers the Review/Signoff Phase. Each of these documents is discussed in detail in the chapters that follow.

Concept

This is where the idea of the initiative is formed. Someone, or some group, has recognized the need for a change and has been motivated to begin the process of implementing it. This phase includes preliminary, often informal discussions with those impacted by the initiative. The individual or group that has initiated the concept will also begin to identify the key team members that should be involved in the project as well as more formal discussions with upper management for funding and support.

Budgeting

The budget is the planned amount of money to be spent on a project. The budget may also outline when the money will be spent. Most organizations have an established budgeting process. Most of these involve an estimate of the number of hours needed to complete the tasks involved and the billing cost per hour (labor), plus the cost of items purchased for the project (fuel, equipment, facilities, etc). Some organizations separate the hourly portion into internal hours (hours worked by employees) and external hours (hours provided by consultants or contract employees). Money spent on personnel to complete tasks on a project is usually expensed. That is, the money is paid immediately and entered as an expense in the accounting system.

The cost of items purchased for the project may be considered expenses or capital expenditures. Expenses are routine costs for items used in the completion of the project. These can include supplies and services. These items are entered as expenses.

Capital is money used to purchase equipment or facilities that become assets of the company. These items can be depreciated. The expenditures are entered into the accounting system as capital and the periodic depreciation is entered as an expense. Depreciation is the amount of value an asset looses in a specific period of time.

The budget for a project combines the estimates of expense and capital and may provide a schedule defining when the money will be spent. This will assist the group funding the project anticipate when the funds must be available.

The project budget is a key factor in building a justification for a project. (See Chapter Three)

Approach

The approach outlines how the initiative will be carried out. It briefly describes the steps that will be taken and the methodology that will be applied. A high-level project plan should be developed, though there may not be enough information to develop a detailed plan at this time.

Below are two approaches that might be used in building a home:

A	B
Identify Location	Identify Builder
Develop Requirements (Based on location)	Develop Requirements
Identify Builder	Identify Location (Based on requirements)
Finalize Design	Finalize Design

Both of these approaches achieve the desired result. Different circumstances and priorities demand different approaches. What is crucial to the project process is not specifically *which* approach is chosen, but that *an* approach is chosen and agreed upon by the team.

Scope

The scope defines the boundaries of the project. It is a detailed listing of what is within the limits of the initiative. Just as crucial is a listing of the elements that are not within the limits of the initiative. The scope eliminates confusion as to what the team is working on .

Failure to clearly define the areas to be impacted results in a fatal situation known as "Scope Creep". Scope Creep is the addition of elements to the project after it has begun. These added deliverables strain project resources and ultimately threaten the team's ability to deliver on time and on budget. A good example of scope creep is a trip to the local shopping mall. If the goal of the trip is to purchase shoelaces and the result is several bags of merchandise, the trip is a victim of scope creep. It is safe to assume that the bags of merchandise exceeded the budget and timeline of the shoelace purchase .

The importance of establishing a scope and holding to it cannot be stressed enough!

An example from home building is the curb and sidewalk along the street in front of the house. The builder must determine if this falls within their responsibility. If so, they must be included in the scope of the project and their cost estimate. If not, the builder will not complete them and will not bill the client for them.

Requirements

Requirements frame the concept into specific deliverables. The definition of the requirements for a project is one of the key factors in its potential success. The requirements define what the project will enable. They establish the expectations of those impacted by the project. *Those who will be impacted must participate in defining the requirements.* These are the areas that will benefit from the initiative; therefore, they know what will be needed to make the project a success. Requirements must be detailed, documented, defined and agreed upon by those impacted.

Failure to document requirements accurately and thoroughly can result in delivery of a product that differs from what was need and/or requested.

There are a number of approaches to developing requirements. Individual meetings with stakeholders may be appropriate, or group meetings of cross-functional representatives may work. What ever approach is used, the requirements of all of the stakeholders must be integrated and approved by the stakeholder group.

In many cases, *high level requirements* are developed to assist in estimating the budget and *detailed requirements* are provided to assist in the design.

In building a home, this phase is where the specifications of the home are defined. High level requirements are those needed by the architect. These include square footage, number of bedrooms, the number of bathrooms, etc. Detailed requirements are needed by the builder. These include floor coverings, light fixtures, doorknobs, etc.

Design

The design identifies how the requirements will be met. It specifically lists the deliverables of the project and how they will fulfill the requirements. Design elements include process flows, a description of the physical environment and any other factors that impact the desired outcome.

The design function is usually carried out by experts in the physical environment. Design documents tend to be very technical in nature.

While the design is usually very technical, it should be reviewed by the stakeholders to ensure that their requirements are met. The presentation to stakeholders should focus on the functionality of the design, rather than the technical aspects. (The stakeholders may more concerned with *what* is being delivered then *how* it is being delivered)

In building a home, the architect works with the client to develop a floor plan that meets their needs. While the plan includes plumbing and structural specifications, the client may be more interested in square footage and convenience.

Build

This is the phase where the design work is turned into physical changes. Equipment is acquired, programs are written, facilities are built, whatever the project calls for. Progress through this phase must be monitored to identify deviation from the timeline and budget. Testing is a critical part of the build phase.

The build phase is complete when the initiative is tested and ready for implementation.

In building a home, the build phase includes all the tasks involved in the actual construction of the home, as defined by the scope.

Implement

After the build phase is complete, the initiative is put into production. This is the Implementation. It may be the use of a new process or system, the introduction of a new product or the launch of a campaign.

In some cases the implementation may be a major portion of the project plan. Steps can include physically moving to a new location, changing systems, changing procedures and training staff.

Implementation in home building is when the client moves into the home.

Review/Signoff

When an initiative has been implemented and is in production, the project team should review and evaluate various aspects of the project. The purpose of the review is to identify aspects of the process that could be improved and document learnings created by the project experience.

♦ Were the goals of the project met?

♦ What goals were not met and why not?

♦ What was the deviation from budget?

♦ What is the explanation of the deviation?

♦ Was the project complete on or before the delivery date?

♦ If the project was not delivered on or before the delivery date, why not?

♦ Was the project management process effective?

♦ How could the project management process be improved?

Execution of a formal sign-off document officially ends a project.

In our home building example, the builder may meet with the client to establish the level of satisfaction with home building experience.

Summary

The project process is designed to guide a team of subject matter experts to their desired result. The process is the same regardless of the type or size of the project. The process is a systematic methodology that assists groups in completing initiatives on time, on budget and with the desired functionality.

Chapter Two

Project Organization

Project Organization

Who is involved in managing a project? The successful management of an initiative requires the cooperation of individuals at many levels within the company. All layers of management play a role in developing and completing a project. Each member of the team has a defined role and strong dependencies can exist between the team members and managers. The terms and titles used in this chapter are meant to be generic. Each company may use different titles, but the responsibilities will be similar.

The responsibilities of each of the positions described in this chapter must be accounted for on every project. On larger projects, separate individuals may be assigned to each role. On smaller projects a single individual may take on the responsibilities of more than one position.

The roles of a typical project team include:

- Project Sponsor
- Program Manager
- Project Leader
- Project Manager
- Project Coordinator
- Team Members
- Design Team
- Stakeholders

The responsibilities of each team member must be made clear from the beginning of the project. This ensures that all the required tasks are covered and avoids duplication of effort.

Project Sponsor

The project sponsor is a senior executive of the company and represents the area of the business that has initiated the project. Often the project sponsor is the manager of the area that is funding the project. Responsibilities of the sponsor include:

- Providing the vision that drives the project goals
- Championing the project within the organization
- Securing the cooperation of other areas within the organization
- Assisting in identifying and gaining commitment from team members
- Assisting in the resolution of issues that involve resources outside of the project team
- Securing project funding
- Approving project goals and deliverables
- Reviewing project status
- Approving changes to the project
- Approving project completion (Signoff)

The sponsor must be active in the launch of the project. The expertise and vision of the sponsor will drive the goals and approach of the project team. The project sponsor may or may not play an active role in the day to day operations of the project. Many sponsors leave the details to the project leader or project manager. The sponsor may review periodic status reports to keep abreast of the progress of the project and intervene when they feel it is appropriate.

Project Leader

The project leader acts as the sponsor's representative. The project leader has decision authority and can be an escalation point for issues and conflicts. The leader must have a strong background in the subject of the project and have sufficient authority within the organization to implement the decisions that are made.

Responsibilities of the leader:

- Act as sponsor's representative on the project team
- Secure the cooperation of other areas within the organization
- Assist in identifying and gaining commitment from team members
- Assist in the resolution of issues that involve resources from other areas
- Approve project goals and deliverables
- Review project status
- Approve changes to the project
- Approve project completion (Signoff)

Program Manager

A Program is a group of projects that contribute to a common goal or are carried out by a single organization. The program manager coordinates the efforts of these various projects. The program manager can assist in developing project plans by representing the interests of all of the projects in the program.

Responsibilities of the program manager:

- Ensure coordination between all projects within the program
- Create and distribute program documents
- Review and approve project documents
- Inform the sponsor of the progress of the projects within the program
- Review proposed changes in project scope, schedule and deliverables
- Review deliverables as completed
- Assist in issue resolution across the program
- Signoff on project completion

Not all projects are part of a program and therefore not all projects have a Program Manager. The Program Manager must be well versed in organization, documentation and communication. First hand knowledge of the subject is helpful, but not required.

Project Manager

The project manager is accountable for the successful completion of all project deliverables.

Responsibilities of the Project Manager:

- Create and distribute project documents
- Coordinate and facilitate project meetings
- Coordinate activities of project team members
- Assign tasks and issues to the project team members
- Resolve issues and obtain decisions as needed to ensure successful completion of the project
- Review deliverables as completed
- Manage and report on project progress

The project manager's major responsibility is coordinating the efforts of the project team to fulfill the vision of the sponsor. The project manager is the communication center for the project. The project manager is responsible for keeping all interested parties aware of the progress of the project. He or she must ensure that the resources assigned to the project are used efficiently and effectively.

As with the program manager, the project manager is not required to have in-depth knowledge of the subject of the project. The project manager must be an expert in the project process. Project managers must possess the traits and attributes necessary to keep the team organized, informed and focused on the project goals.

Project Coordinator

The project coordinator assists the project manager in documenting, communicating and coordinating the project efforts. On large projects, the project manager may need assistance in documenting meetings, issues and task updates. A project coordinator can provide the administrative assistance necessary to keep the project documentation updated and ensure that information is communicated effectively. This is especially true in cases when the sponsor is acting as project manager. The sponsor may have responsibilities beyond the management of a project. The coordinator can relieve the sponsor/manager of much of the administrative tasks associated with project management.

Responsibilities of a project coordinator:

- Creating and maintaining project documents
- Scheduling and coordinating meetings
- Distributing project documents
- Creating meeting summaries

The project coordinator must be familiar with the project process. He or she must have exceptional organization and communication skills. The coordinator's main responsibility is to support the project manager, allowing the manager to devote more time to the project team and ensure that the deliverables are met.

Project Team

Members of the project team are responsible for the execution of the project plan according to the established timeline. The project team is made up of individuals who represent various areas that contribute to the project deliverables. Team members are the subject matter experts that will develop and execute the project plan with the assistance of the project manager.

Team members must have a level of expertise that allows them to competently represent their subject area. They must also have sufficient authority within that area to bring additional resources to the project if necessary. They must be willing to accept their assigned tasks and any issues that are within their area of expertise.

Responsibilities of the project team:

- Participate in the creation of the Charter and Project Plan
- Complete all assigned tasks
- Resolve issues as assigned
- Act as subject matter expert for their area
- Represent their area in all discussions
- Bring additional resources to the project as necessary
- Alert the project team to any delays in the completion of assigned tasks
- Alert the project team to any issues they discover

The project team executes the plan. They must have the willingness, expertise and resources to complete the plan within the prescribed timeline.

The size of the team varies with the complexity of the project. At least one representative from each area participating in the project should be on the team. Oversized teams can be more difficult to coordinate. If difficulties arise, it may be possible to divide a large project into smaller ones (thus creating a *program*) This will allow more defined planning and allow the teams to focus on their specific deliverables.

Design Team

Certain members of the project team may be asked to organize a team to design the project solution. These team members will have specialized technical knowledge of the subject area. The design team will use the requirements gathered by the project team as a guide to develop the design. In some cases the project team will also serve as the design team.

The design team is also responsible for notifying the project team if there are specific aspects of the design that should be addressed in the requirements. This notification should take place before the requirements are gathered. This allows the project team to address these items in the requirements process rather then return to them after the requirements are gathered.

Responsibilities of the design team:
- Creating a physical solution that fills the project requirements
- Coordinating efforts with the group that is gathering the requirements
- Notifying the project team of design aspects to be addressed in the requirements
- Documenting the design of the solution

Stakeholders

Stakeholders are those individuals and areas that are impacted by the project. Stakeholders are often described as the users of whatever the project is creating. They must take an active part in developing the requirements, completion criteria and success criteria of the project. They should also review the project design and be informed of any changes to the project after the Charter is published. Managers of stakeholder areas should be on the distribution list for all project communications.

Stakeholder responsibilities:
- Participation in the development of project requirements
- Identification of the impacts to their subject area
- Review of project charter
- Review of project design
- Review/Approve project timeline
- Communicate issues to the project manager through their project team representative
- Certain stakeholders may be selected by the team to sign off on the completed project.

Stakeholders are often referred to as "Customers" or "Clients". They should participate in the project process and be kept informed of the project status.

Summary

The organization of a project is a key factor in its success. The successful management of an initiative requires the cooperation of individuals at many levels within the company. Several layers of management may play a role in developing and completing a project. Individuals can fill more than one position on the team.

A typical project organization includes:

- Project Sponsor
- Program Manager
- Project Manager
- Project Coordinator
- Team Members
- Design Team
- Stakeholders

CHAPTER THREE

The Project Charter

The Project Charter

The charter is one of the most critical documents in all project documentation. The charter has such importance that this entire chapter is devoted to it. The project charter outlines what the project is to accomplish and why it is important. It defines how the goals will be reached and when they will be delivered. It is a declaration of the purpose and benefits of the project and establishes the specific deliverables. In short, it is a contract with the stakeholders.

Chapter One addressed the phases of the Project Process. Chapter Two outlined the organization of a project. The Charter documents these items.

In terms of the Project Process, information contained in the Charter refers to the Concept, Budget, Approach and Scope phases.

To break this down further, the charter contains:

Goal Statement
> *A brief statement that describes the objectives of the project*

Executive Summary
> *A brief narrative the describes the project*

Approach
> *A list of the tenets that the team will adhere to*

Scope
> *What is specifically within the scope?*
> *What is specifically NOT within the scope?*

Project Justification
Why is the project important?
How will the business benefit from the project?

Constraints
What limits are placed on the project?

Organization
Who will be involved in the project?
What areas of the company do they represent?

Completion Criteria
What will signify that the project is complete?

Success Criteria
What will signify that the project was a success?

Timeline/Schedule
How long will the project take?
What milestones are associated with the project?

Assumptions & Dependencies
What assumptions were made in developing the Charter?
What is the project team dependent upon for success?
What are the impacts of the failure of these assumptions and dependencies?

Impacts
What other areas within the organization will this project impact?

Change Control Process
What is the process for changing the above items after they are documented?
Who must approve changes?

It is important to note that the charter is a fixed document. Once published it is very difficult to change. The information presented must tell an accurate story, but it cannot be confining. The language of the charter must not be so specific that it limits the ability of the project team to explore alternative solutions. The content of the charter dictates the limits of the project. The language and information must be carefully crafted to define the bounds of the project, but not limit the team's ability to create solutions.

Goal Statement

The goal statement is a sentence or two that defines what the project will accomplish. It is a very high level view of the project. This is often very difficult to craft as team members may have differing ideas on the goal of the project.

The goal statement defines the remainder of the document. It is a reference point when developing the approach and scope of the project. An example is a firm that has decided to use direct mail for the first time. A team is brought together to create the direct mail program. What is the goal of the project?

♦ It could be to determine if direct mail generates more business then other marketing approaches.

♦ It could be to determine if the cost of direct mail is offset by incremental business.

♦ It could be to compare various direct mail methods.

The goal statement defines what the project will do.

Here are examples:

"To produce and mail a direct mail campaign and measure response for comparison to other marketing approaches"

In this case, the team will focus on getting the mail out and measuring response. The team may also develop marketing programs using other delivery methods for comparison. Expense and speed factors are less important. The main thrust of the project will be to deliver the message and measure the response.

"To determine if direct mail results justify direct mail expense"

Expense factors will be a crucial factor in achieving this goal. The team will focus on delivering mail as inexpensively as possible and defining the factors to be used in measuring the results.

"To determine the most profitable method of delivering direct mail"

In this case the team will explore several different methods of creating and delivering direct mail, establish measurement criteria and evaluate the results.

Each of these goals could be logical in the overall directive of creating and delivering direct mail. However, each goal leads to a different approach and requires team members with different skill sets.

The goal of the project must be made clear to everyone involved. This includes the sponsors, leaders, team members, stakeholders and any other interest parties.

Executive Summary

The summary is essentially a summation of all of the other parts of the charter document. It is a brief explanation of what the project will do, why it is important and how it will be accomplished. Brief descriptions of the current and target environments can also be helpful. The executive summary is at a very high level with few details. The reader should be able to review the summary and have a basic understanding of what the project is about.

An Executive Summary should contain:

♦ A brief description of the events that prompted the need for this project
♦ An explanation as to how this project will resolve the situation
♦ Why it is important to resolve the situation (Benefits to the business)
♦ Highlights of the approach that will be taken

Include the items that have been determined as of the time of the writing. If the specific approach us not known, it should be referenced with terms such as: "The current situation and possible approaches will be researched. The final approach will be selected from the alternatives developed in this process".

A proven method to effective executive summaries is to create them last. That is, create all of the other portions of the charter and then summarize them into the Executive Summary. Summaries can vary from a few sentences to several paragraphs, but should rarely exceed a single page.

Approach

As discussed in Chapter One, the Approach outlines the processes the team will use to accomplish the goals of the project. It also establishes guidelines the team will be using in creating and implementing the project plan. For instance, to reduce project expense the team may decide to use existing facilities whenever possible. At the time they are establishing the approach, the team may not know whether existing facilities are available or not, but they can still list this as an operating guideline.

Items that should be included in the approach:

♦ Who will be on the team?

♦ What is the approximate timeline?

♦ Will the project be implemented in phases?

♦ Does this charter cover all phases or just phase one?

♦ What is the content of each phase?

♦ Has the implementation plan been developed?

   ♦ If so, what is it?

   ♦ If not, Who will develop it? When? What are the guidelines?

Here are some examples:

For a project to make improvements to an existing process:

> "A cross-functional team will be assembled to evaluate the current environment and make recommendations for enhancements. The team will be made up of representatives from both the Sales and Servicing areas. Enhancements will be limited to those that can be implemented within 90 days. After identifying the enhancements, an implementation plan will be developed that adheres to the established timeline. Existing facilities and systems will be leveraged whenever possible and contract labor will be kept to a minimum."

For a project to migrate to a new system:

> "Operations will continue on existing facilities until the new system has been installed and tested. Operations will be converted to the new system in phases, starting with the areas of lowest volume and ending with the areas of highest volume. The systems will operate in parallel until all operations have converted. The timeline for completion of all conversions is 120 days from the first conversion to the last. The timeline for individual conversions will vary with the complexity of the conversion and the volume involved."

Scope

The scope section of the charter documents the bounds of the project as described in Chapter One. There are two major items that should be addressed in the scope section of the charter document: Items that are in scope and items that are out of scope. The purpose of defining a scope is to eliminate confusion as to what the project will do and what it will not do. This is key to managing the expectations of the stakeholders.

Detail and clarity of the scope are crucial. Specific systems, processes and/or facilities should be listed. Cumulative or generic terms can be used as long as there is a universal understanding of the limits of the statement. In a homebuilding example, the phrase "all plumbing within the structure" can be used rather then listing all of the individual components of the plumbing of a house.

Items within the scope define the design and final budget of the project. Once established and agreed upon by all parties, the scope cannot be changed without evaluating the ramifications of the change and approving the new scope with all parties. Adding to a project scope without evaluating the ramifications (a condition known as "scope creep") has been the downfall for many initiatives. The skill sets of the team members and the plans of the team are centered on the scope as defined in the charter. Additions to scope may bring in tasks that the team is not equipped or staffed to handle. This places the project timeline deliverables and budget in jeopardy.

Equally important as the listing of items in scope is a listing of the items that are NOT in scope. This is instrumental in avoiding confusion as to what the project will deliver. "Not In Scope" should include items that may be assumed by those outside the team to be part of the initiative. In a project to convert from one system to another, creation of the new system may or may not be within scope.

Project Justification

Why are we doing this? How will the results of this project benefit us? There can be a number of answers to these questions. Most of these fall into two categories: Financial and Non-financial.

Financial Benefits

> Note: The purpose of this section is to explain the logic behind the documentation of the financial benefits of a project. This is not meant as an in depth explanation of financial concepts. These examples are simplified to demonstrate reporting, rather than content. The terms used in this section are intended to be generic. (This is an example of *defining scope* and *managing expectations*)

Financial benefits enhance the profitability of the organization. Most projects have some type of financial implications. Projects that improve customer service lead to more repeat customers. More repeat customers lead to reduced sales expense (Under the theory the repeat customers are easier to sell than new customers are). Reduced sales expense leads to higher profitability. The launch of a new product leads to increased sales, which leads to increased revenue, which leads to higher profits. A new employee benefit may reduced attrition, which in turn reduces hiring expense. The list goes on.

The challenge in building the financial justification of a project is in quantifying the impacts of the project. The impacts are generally the cost of the project compared to the improvement in profitability (Increased revenue or reduced expenses).

The cost of the project can be divided into two types. *Capital* is money used to purchase facilities that can be depreciated over time such as buildings, equipment or software. *Expense* is the non-capital cost of the project. This includes personnel costs, legal fees, travel, supplies, etc. Estimates of these costs can usually be obtained from those that are doing the work.

Expense reductions can be easily defined. Replacing an inefficient system will result in a quantifiable reduction in expense. These reductions can usually be accurately predicted.

Increased revenue can be more difficult to define. These are often based on assumptions. Revenue increases based on increased sales are a good example. If increased revenue is dependent upon increased sales, there is an assumption that sales will increase as a result of the project. Care must be taken to justify the assumed increase in sales.

The timeframe for a project justification varies from one company to another. Most firms use a three to five year projection. The financial justification is the difference between the anticipated costs and the estimated benefits. The measures used by the company are then applied to the justification argument. There are a number of measurement theories. Examples are return on assets, return on equity and payback period. The company's financial standards may use "net present value" in these calculations. Refer to your company's policy for the method to be used and to ensure that this information is reported properly.

The project justification that is contained in the charter needn't be overly detailed. The purpose of this section is to give the stakeholders a high level view of the benefits of the project. Quite often the financial justification has been completed and approved prior to the initiation of the project. The charter document should reflect the information the decision was based on.

Below is an example of a financial justification that impacts both revenue and expenses. This example is the cash flow generated by the launch of a new product:

Cash Flow Analysis				
Costs:			Revenues:	
Initiation			Sales	
Capital (one-time)	$2,000,000		Year One	$2,700,000
(Hardware, Software, Facilities)			(*15,000 units @ $200-10% sales expense)	
Expense (one-time)			Years Two thru Five	14,400,000
(2000 hours @ $100 per hour)	200,000		(20,000 units/yr @ $200-10% sales expense)	
Total Initiation	$2,200,000			
Annual				
Maintenance	50,000			
(Incremental to existing)				
Depreciation				
(10-Year Straight Line)	200,000			
Total Annual	$250,000			
Five Year Total	$1,250,000			
Production Costs				
Year One	1,500,000			
(15,000 units @ $100)				
Years Two thru Five	8,000,000			
(20,000 units/yr @ $100)				
Five Year Production	$9,500,000			
Marketing Expense				
Year One	$500,000			
Years Two thru Five	1,000,000			
Five Year Marketing	1,500,000			
Total for Five Years	14,450,000			17,100,000
Five Year Cash Flow	$2,650,000			

*Sales figures based on marketing study available upon request

Is $2,650,000 enough to justify the project? The company's financial policies will dictate the answer.

This example uses "cash flow". Financial policies of some companies may require the use of another method, such as net present value. The company's policies should be consulted to ensure that the proper method is used.

Below is an example for a project that impacts only expenses. This particular example is the cash flow resulting from the implementation of a process to reduce production cost.

Cash Flow Analysis			
Costs:		Production Savings:	
Initiation			
Capital (one-time)	$2,000,000	Years One thru Five	$6,250,000
(Equipment, Facilities)		(*50,000 units @ $25 savings per unit)	
Expense			
(2000 hours @ $100 per hour)	200,000		
Total Initiation	$2,200,000		
Annual			
Maintenance	50,000		
(Incremental to existing)			
Depreciation	200,000		
(10-Year Straight Line)			
Total Annual	$250,000		
Five Year Total	$1,250,000		
Total for Five Years	3,450,000		6,250,000
Five Year Cash Flow	$2,800,000		
*Assumes current production levels continue			

*Assumes current production levels continue

Once again, the company's financial policies will determine if $2,800,000 justifies the project.

Non-Financial Benefits

There can be various benefits to a project that are difficult to quantify in terms of dollars and cents. Among these are projects to bring the company in compliance with a new regulatory requirement or the resolution of a safety issue.

Many financial benefits are rooted in less clearly definable non-financial benefits. Improvements to an outdated facility may reduce employee attrition or increase productivity by providing a more comfortable work environment. Compliance with new regulations avoids fines (which can be defined in financial terms) and avoids negative publicity (which is more difficult to define)

Both financial and non-financial benefits are listed in the charter.

Constraints

This section provides information on the limits imposed on the project. This section should detail the constraints and why they exist. For example, "All work must be completed prior to the holiday shut-down which begins December 15 and continues until January 5." The constraints will have a profound impact on the scope and completion criteria. Items that cannot be completed within the constraints should not be included in the scope. Constraints can be in terms of budget, timeline, resources or any other aspect of the project.

Many projects may not have constraints. In this case this section may be omitted or the lack of constraints noted in the text. ("No constraints have been identified at this time.")

Organization

This section of the charter lists all of the positions within the project team and the resources that have been identified to fill those roles. Note positions that have yet to be filled. This will acknowledge that the need for that position has been recognized, even if the resource has not been identified. The charter should list the sponsor of the project, the project manager and any other parties that have committed to the effort and the role and responsibility that each individual has accepted.

The positions should be listed by title rather then by the individual's name. The membership of the project team may change through the course of the project. Using titles will eliminate the need to re-draft the charter with each change in personnel. The individuals that are filling specific roles should be listed once. This will allow the text to be amended more easily than if the names are used throughout the document.

Completion Criteria

How will we know when the project is complete? What physical evidence will demonstrate that the work has been completed?

The completion criteria determine when all of the tasks associated with the project have been completed. There must be some physical evidence that the job is done. This is known as the evidence of completion. This evidence could be a document that is delivered to the sponsor or the delivery of the first unit of a new product. These criteria must be determined prior to the launch of the project. Failure to identify the criteria for the completion of the project may result in scope creep as the project continues beyond its original timeline.

Completion criteria can be an extension of the approach. It is the physical evidence that the steps needed to complete the approach have been accomplished.

The criteria for the completion of a project are often described as a list of specific deliverables. When all the deliverables have been fulfilled, the project is complete.

Success Criteria

There is a distinct difference between Success Criteria and Completion Criteria. A project is complete when all of the deliverables associated with the project are fulfilled. A project is a success when the goals of the project have been achieved.

An example to demonstrate this point is a marathon runner. The runner's project (the race) is complete when they cross the finish line. The project (race) is a success if the runner has achieved their pre-determined goal, whether it be in terms of the amount of time it took to complete the race, what place they finished or any other measurement they have selected.

It is entirely possible to complete an unsuccessful project. However, very few incomplete projects are successful.

Success criteria can be derived from the goal statement and project justification. In the case of the new product referred to in the project justification section, the project will be complete when the product is available. It will be a success when the financial rewards of the project are realized.

Success criteria can be documented in several ways. Specific items can be selected as the measures of success. The items selected must be clearly identified and easily measured. Ease of measurement is a key factor. Results of the project must be easily identified and demonstrated.

The details of the items can be entered into a matrix to demonstrate the results before and after the project.

Below is an example using a project to reduce both production time and cost per unit:

	Current Environment	Target Environment
Time of production (From initiation to delivery to the warehouse)	8 Production Hours	6 Production Hours
Average Cost of Production (Total production expense divided by the number of units produced)	$120	$100

In this case, the project is considered a success if the time of production and cost of production match the target environment.

Timeline/Schedule

It is important that the project charter include information about the timeline associated with a project. This is not meant to be a detailed project plan, but rather a high level reflection of the time required to complete the project. Even something as basic as "*It is estimated that this project will be completed within 90 days of approval*" can suffice.

Whatever information is known when the charter is developed should be included. Tables are often used to display the timeline. The steps of the project process described in Chapter One can be used as the initial milestones. A *milestone* is a key point of measurement in the progress of the project.

Milestone	Target Date
Project Launch	February 1
Approach/Scope defined	February 14
Requirements Documented	March 10
Design Complete	April 1
Build Complete	May 15
Implementation	May 31

The goal of this section is to provide an estimate of the time frame for the project. A detailed project plan is not necessary at this stage.

Assumptions and Dependencies

Project teams are often dependent upon the outcome of other initiatives or the efforts of another area. The team may make certain assumptions in developing their plans. Assumptions and dependencies impact the completion of the project as described in the Completion Criteria and/or the success of the project as described in the Success Criteria. This section of the charter documents dependencies and assumptions. This section also identifies the impacts of the failure of an assumption or dependency.

In the example of building a home, the project timeline may be dependent upon the construction of roads or bridges. The team building the home may not responsible for building the road or the bridge, thus they are dependent upon it.

Examples of assumptions are economic factors, weather, availability of resources and competition. Examples of dependencies include the installation of a new system, the relocation of operations or the hiring of qualified staff.

Impacts

This section of the charter identifies how this project will affect areas of the company that are not directly involved in the project. If a technical team is developing a new system, the employees that use this system are not directly involved in the project, but are impacted by it. The impacted areas may need to alter their procedures to accommodate the new system. They may also need to schedule training for their employees. Production may be impacted by the installation of the new system Employees may be removed from production for training and a output may slow while employees become familiar with the new environment. A project can also impact other projects by diverting resources.

A project may eliminate a manual process or reduce the effort required to complete a task. It may also change a process that another area is dependent upon and that area must be aware of the change so they can accommodate for it. All impacts to areas that are not involved in the project should be listed.

Change Control

The charter must make some provision for changes to the project goal, scope and/or deliverables. While these changes should be extremely rare, the charter should make allowances for the situation, should it arise.

The area of the company that is providing funding for the project must review and approve any changes to the charter. Also, the stakeholders should be notified of any such changes, as their areas may be dependent upon the project of other initiatives.

Changes to the charter can be documented in two ways. (1)They can be listed in an addendum to the original charter. In this case the original charter is not altered and the changes are noted and approved in a separate document. (2)Re-write and re-approve the original charter, thus creating another version of the original. In either case, the new document must be distributed to and approved by all impacted areas.

The most common change to a charter is the timeline. Issues identified in the project can delay the final delivery date. These changes are often addressed in the charter as needing the approval of the management group, but do not require a re-draft of the charter document.

Provisions can be made for changes that do not require approval. For example, the charter may allow budget increases of 5% without approval or delays in the timeline of up to 3 days. These provisions will avoid the necessity of securing approval for small changes. NOTE: These provisions should only be used on projects that have the necessary flexibility. It is not be appropriate on all projects.

General Comments

The charter document is the "Constitution" of a project. While the document must be thorough, it needn't be cumbersome. Quite often a template can be used to create the document. In the template, some language (such as "Roles and Responsibilities" and "Change Management") can be standardized, with only the information specific to the project being added.

The charter document should be finalized by the project team. The team must endorse the contents of the document and sincerely believe that the results described in the document are attainable.

Summary

The project charter defines the purpose of the project, who will carry it out and when and how it will be completed. Key elements of the charter include:

Goal Statement
Executive Summary
Approach
Scope
Project Justification
Constraints

Organization
Completion Criteria
Success Criteria
Timeline/Schedule
Assumptions & Dependencies
Impacts
Change Control Process

The charter should be developed by the project team and approved by the governing bodies.

Once established, the items listed in the charter become binding and can only be changed by implementing the change control process.

CHAPTER 4

Project Documentation

Project Documents

Comments on Project Documents

There are essentially two types of documents that are created to support a project. These are Fixed documents, which do not change after they are published, and Living documents, which can be changed on a regular basis.

Examples of fixed documents are charters and status reports. The charter establishes the specific deliverables associated with the project. It also defines the project budget and timeline. Once published, it creates the identity of the project and establishes the expectations of the stakeholders. Any change to the charter after it is published will result in changes to the timeline, budget and/or the deliverables. The charter should not be changed without proper consideration of the impacts of the change. In most cases, a major change to a project's deliverables will require that a new charter be drafted.

Once circulated, a status report communicates a current snapshot of the project. It relates the situation as it exists at the time it is created. Changes in the condition of the project may change, but the condition at a particular time does not.

An issue list is an example of a living document. Issues are added as they are identified, their status tracked and resolution noted. This document could change daily.

Version Management

Version management assures that all parties are working with the most recent version of a document. Noting the date of the most recent change to the document is a common method of version management. The document "footer" is a convenient way to record the last revision on a document. In most word processing programs, the footer can automatically record the last time the document was changed.

It is also important to note the individuals who are authorized to revise documents. The "official" version can only be revised by those who are authorized to do so.

Language

Project documents must be written in a clear and understandable tone. The documents will be reviewed by individuals that may not have in-depth knowledge of the subject or may not be able to monitor the project status on a regular basis. The language used should be free of jargon or jargon should be explained when it is used.

Proper grammar, punctuation and sentence structure will give documents a feeling of credibility. SPELLING COUNTS: A document filled with misspellings will lack credibility to the reader.

Templates

After the format of a document has been finalized, the headings and standard text can be used to create a template for future use. This same template can be applied to many types of projects with only the project-specific information being added.

Types of Documentation

The documents associated with a project include:

♦ The project charter (See Chapter 2)
♦ The approach document (project methodology)
♦ Meeting summaries (the results of meetings)

- The project plan (the project plan and milestones)
- The design document (the design of the solution)
- The issues list (the issues discovered and resolved during the project)
- Status reports (the status of the project at certain points in time)
- The Signoff Document (The agreement that the project has been completed)

The distribution of these documents varies with the information contained and the impacts of the project. The distribution list should be created as the charter and project plans are being developed.

Some documents require approval. Notably the charter and the signoff will be of particular interest to most of the parties involved in the project.

Documentation Responsibilities

The steps in creating project documents include:

- Definition of the content of the document
- Creation of the document
- Maintenance of the document
- Approval of the document
- Distribution of the document

The table below provides a high-level view of these responsibilities. They are discussed in more detail in the following pages. *Note: "Approval" denotes an official review and signature. "Distribution" refers to circulating the document to a specific group outside of the project team. All documents should be discussed with the project team prior to distribution.*

Document	Content	Creation	Approval	Maintenance	Distribution
Charter	Project Team	Project Manager	Project Sponsor, Key Stakeholders	N/A	Project Manager, Project Sponsor
Approach Document	Project Team	Project Manager	Project Sponsor, Key Stakeholders	N/A	Project Manager, Project Sponsor
Project Plan	Project Team	Project Manager	N/A	Project Manager	N/A
Design	Design Team within Project Team	Design Team within Project Team	Project Team, Key Stakeholders	Design Team within Project Team	N/A
Issues	Project Team	Project Manager	N/A	Project Manager	Project Manager
Status Reports	Project Manager	Project Manager	N/A	N/A	Project Manager
Signoff	Project Team	Project Manager	Project Sponsor, Key Stakeholders	N/A	Project Manager

Approach Document

A document detailing the methodology that a team is applying to an initiative can be useful in communicating objectives and managing expectations. The approach document is a detailed version of the "Approach" section of the project charter. Quite often the details of the approach have not been established when the charter is written. An approach document can be distributed to the stakeholders after the team has had an opportunity to review the requirements and develop their approach. This is another example of a document that can be used to avoid confusion as to what the project team intends to do.

The approach document should be distributed to the same individuals that received the project charter.

The approach document is a fixed document. Once published it should not be changed. If changes do take place, a revised approach must be created and distributed.

Meeting Summaries

The results of meetings must be communicated to all interested parties. This group generally includes the meeting attendees, the project manager, anyone impacted by the outcome and anyone that has requested the information.

Meeting summaries are create to:

♦ Ensure a common understanding of the results of the meeting

♦ Provide documentation of decisions that were made in the meeting

♦ Clearly communicate deliverables that were assigned in the meeting

This has traditionally been accomplished through the distribution of meeting minutes. Minutes are a detailed account of what happened in the meeting. They describe the meeting in great detail, even reporting what was said and by whom. This document can be described as a "paraphrased transcript".

Minutes are necessary in many types of meetings, particularly when legal matters are discussed, but are far too demanding and cumbersome for most projects. They are demanding because they require one of the meeting attendees to be dedicated to writing down everything that happens. This can put a resource constraint on the project team. It forces a team member to concentrate on scribing rather then participating in the meeting. Often an additional resource must be brought in to take on the responsibility. Minutes are cumbersome in that the recipients of the document must sift through a great deal of text to find the key points of the meeting.

Meeting summaries are a much more efficient way to communicate the results of a meeting. A summary documents only the key points and omits much of the text found in meeting minutes. Summaries are easier to create and much easier to read.

Summaries should include:

- The date, time and title or purpose of the meeting
- A list of attendees
- The topics discussed and the results of the discussion
  - Reports presented
  - Review of project plan
  - Review of open issues

- Decisions
- A list of deliverables, the individuals responsible and when the deliverables are due
- Information on future meetings

The meeting facilitator or project manager can produce a meeting summary from their notes. If a project coordinator is used, he or she can create the summary as the meeting progresses. Summaries should be created and distributed as soon after the meeting as possible.

Meeting summaries are considered fixed documents. However, they can be corrected if errors are discovered.

Project Plan

The project plan (sometimes referred to as a "Task Plan") details the specific tasks that must be completed to deliver the project. The plan describes the *task* (a specific item to be completed), its *duration* (the amount of time required to complete the task), its *resources* (who is responsible for completing the task) and if the task has any *dependencies* (tasks that must be completed before this one). The tasks on which other tasks are dependent are called *predecessors*.

Each task must have *evidence of completion*. Evidence of completion is a tangible sign that the task has been completed. This can be a report, a process, a product, what ever the task is intended to produce.

In terms of the Project Process discussed in Chapter One, the Project Plan pertains to the Requirements, Design, Build and Implementation phases.

The project plan establishes the timeline and specific deliverables for the project. The end results of the project plan are the deliverables defined in the "Completion Criteria" section of the charter. The plan is the standard that the status is measured against. There are two types of project plans: the High Level Plan and the Detail Plan.

The high level plan summarizes tasks to create the project timeline. The detail plan breaks the summary tasks into individual items. The timeline of the summary plan may be several weeks or months. It is difficult to make detailed plans months in advance of the actual event and, even if it were easy to plan that far in advance, the tasks would most likely change in the interim.

The project plan is a living document. It will change as tasks are completed and additional tasks are discovered. Additional tasks are not considered "changes" to the project in themselves. Project plans are developed to cover the entire timeline of the project. As the team works through the project, details of tasks are uncovered and added to the plan. This allows the plan to accurately reflect the work being done and allows the team the flexibility to adjust their plans as they become more familiar with the tasks.

Project plans are organized into *Milestones* . Milestones mark the completion of a major event in the project. Within each milestone are the tasks that lead to its completion.

Tasks are either *concurrent* or *dependent*. Concurrent tasks can be completed at the same time. Dependent tasks must be completed in order. Tasks may be dependent because one task employs the outcome of another or because the same resources are needed to complete both. A task on which another task is dependent is known as a *predecessor*.

Every task listed in a project plan must be a predecessor to another task or result in a final deliverable. If a task is neither a predecessor nor a deliverable, there is a question as to whether the task is within the scope of the project. If it is not within scope, the team should not devote resources to it.

Project plans must address all of the deliverables listed in the "Completion Criteria" of the charter. The project plan lists the steps necessary to deliver the functionality described in the charter. The plan must list all of the tasks needed to complete all of the deliverables.

The project plan is a living document. Tasks may be added are issues are addressed or details are uncovered.

Using Software

There are a number of excellent software programs available to assist in developing project plans. These are very useful tools and should be employed to their fullest extent. Training on the specific software to be used is essential. Most software packages can be learned in as little as a few hours and will provide invaluable planning and management assistance.

Requirements Document

This document details the expectations of the stakeholders in the project. The requirements specify exactly what the project must deliver to achieve the goals described in the charter. Requirements must be detailed and complete. The format of the requirements document will vary with the type of project. At a minimum it should list the specific deliverables and functionality needed. As discussed in Chapter One, the individuals who have initiated the project must be the driving force in developing the requirements.

Any aspect that is not specifically addressed in the requirements will be left to the discretion of the designers. The designers will use their own criteria in making design decisions if not guided by a specific requirement. The group that is defining the requirements can comfortably leave some details to the designers. However, there will be cases where the criteria of the designers will differ from those of the stakeholders. The project manager must make every effort to identify these cases and address them with both teams prior to the finalization of the requirements.

Note that detailed requirements are not necessarily voluminous. They are merely complete. Thorough requirements can be documented in a single line or many pages.

Once agreed upon, the requirements document is a fixed document. Changes to the requirements after approval will often impact the design and implementation.

Design Document

The design is the technical solution to the situation that prompted the project. It can feature flow charts, text, blueprints, schematics, whatever is appropriate for the area involved. Whatever format is used, the design must contain detailed specifications. The design may cause a revision of the budget, or the budget may cause a revision of the design.

Features of the design should be reviewed with key stakeholders. As mentioned earlier, the stakeholders may not be as interested in the technical features of the design as they are in the functionality it provides.

Issues

An issue is an unexpected event or circumstance that impacts the project. The issues document is used to track and monitor these items to their resolution. The resolution of an issue is the steps or tasks necessary to remove the barriers to completion created by the issue.

The document itself can be in a spreadsheet format. The title section of the document should include the name of the project and the date of the report. The title section should also include a running total of the number of issues. The rows of the sheet are the individual issues that the team has uncovered. The columns of the sheet contain information pertaining to each issue. The columns generally include:

- ◆ The number used to identify the issue
- ◆ The name of the issue
- ◆ A brief description of the issue
- ◆ The impact of the issue (Does it delay the timeline, threaten functionality, etc)
- ◆ The name of the person responsible for the resolution
- ◆ The expected date of resolution
- ◆ Notes on the status and/or resolution of the issue

The Issues Document (Sometimes referred to as the "Issues List") is a living document. It may change several times a day. The ability to update the "Official" version of the document should be limited to those with an over-all view of the projects, usually the project manager or a member of their staff. The document should be distributed on a pre-established schedule to all team members.

Issues can have one of two statuses: *Open* and *Closed.* An Open issue has been identified, but the resolution of the issue is still in development. After the resolution has been identified, the tasks necessary to implement the resolution must be added to the project plan and the impacts of these additional tasks calculated, including the assignment of resources.

To close an issue requires that the resolution be identified, implementation of the resolution be planned and all interested parties be informed of the impacts on the project timeline, budget and deliverables. The issue can be closed prior to the actual implementation of the resolution. The item is no longer an issue when a resolution has been identified and an implementation plan developed. The *issue* has then been transformed into a series of *tasks*. These tasks should be added to the project plan.

The issues document should be divided into two sections. The first section should list only open issues with the resource assigned, the due date, comments on the current situation and the impact of the issue. The second section should contain only closed issues. This provides a record of issues and how they were resolved. The comment section on a closed issue should contain information on how the issue was resolved and the impacts of the resolution.

As issues are closed, they are transferred from the "Open" section of the documents to the "Closed" section. As the list grows, it can become difficult to assign identification numbers to new issues. The running total in the title section can be helpful in assigning issue numbers as it will define what the next available number is.

The project sponsor and/or stakeholders may be interested in the issues that the team is dealing with. However, the entire list may be too cumbersome for them. In this case, a separate, smaller list can be created for distribution to this group. This list contains only the most significant issues. The criteria for the issues that are contained on this list can be established at the beginning of the project. The criteria might be that an issue must threaten the timeline and/or the resolution may require the intervention of an area outside of the project team. The project sponsor and stakeholders should decide what issues they are interested in reviewing. The "short list" should also have a pre-established circulation schedule. It can also be included in the status report.

Status

The status report outlines the current health of the project. It essentially defines the progress of the project in comparison to project plan, provides information on delays or issues and provides any other information of use to the distribution audience. Status reports are used to communicate information on the project to individuals that may not be directly involved with the project on a daily basis. Because of this, the report must be detailed enough that the entire audience understands the current situation, yet at a high enough level that the report is clear to all concerned.

Because the status report may be the only periodic outbound communication from the project team, it is crucial that the format and content communicate effectively. Once published, a status report is a fixed document.

Project Status

There are several methods to report overall project status. All involve a series of words, numbers or phrases with pre-established definitions that are used to describe the health of the project.

An example is "Red-Yellow-Green". In this example, a project that is "Green" is on schedule with no major issues, a project in "Yellow" has issues that potentially impact the timeline, deliverables and/or budget. "Yellow" projects can be slightly behind schedule, but should recover in time to deliver all functionality on the target date. A project in "Red" has serious issues that threaten the functionality, timeline, budget or any combination of these. The criteria that describes each of these status codes must be defined so that all concerned parties have a common understanding of their meanings.

Similar scales can be established using the key drivers of the project. Examples include "Ahead of schedule, On schedule, Behind schedule"; "Under budget, On budget, Over budget", among others. The key is to make the status meaningful to the audience.

Adjustments can be made to status with revisions to timeline, budget, etc. For example, if an issue arises that delays the project delivery beyond the provisions of the charter, but does not impact the budget or deliverables, the guidelines may dictate that the project status becomes "Yellow". If the timeline is not revised, the project will remain in "Yellow" status until its completion. This can be confusing to those reviewing the status reports. To remedy this, the project manager may implement the "Change Control" procedures detailed in the project charter document. The project manager can request that the project timeline be adjusted to reflect the revised delivery dates. If a revised timeline is properly approved, the status of the project can be changed to "Green" in the revised situation. This change should be communicated through the status report.

There are many different report formats that can be used, depending on the information needs of the audience.

Below is an example of a weekly status report for a small project that is distributed to a group that is routinely involved in the project process:

Status Report-*Project Name*   *Date of Report*

Goals for this week	▪ Goal One ▪ Goal Two	% Complete/Status % Complete/Status
Goals for next week	▪ Goal One ▪ Goal Two	
Issues	▪ Issue One ▪ Issue Two	
Comments		

In this example, the goals can be copied directly from the project plan. In addition to items from the project plan, "Goals for next week" may contain lagging items that were not completed on schedule. In developing the report for the following week, "Goals for next week" can be inserted into the "Goals for this week" section, with the % Complete/Status noted. The issues listed should be those that explain any delays in completing items listed on the project plan. "Comments" can contain any information that the project manager feels appropriate. This can include milestones achieved or upcoming, issue resolutions, etc.

This example outlines the basic information that should be contained in any status report.

More complex projects may require the addition of information that pertains to the goals and deliverables of the project. This allows those recipients that are not routinely involved with the project to stay fresh on the goals and timeline. The format of this status report is somewhat more complicated, but most of the additional information does not change though the course of the project.

Below is a sample of this type of status report.

Status Report-	*Project Name* *Project Sponsor* *Project Manager*			*Date*
Project Goal Statement				
This Week's Goals	% Complete	Next Week's Goals	Issues	
Comments				
Project Milestones				
Milestone	Original Target Date	Revised Target Date	Status	
Milestone One	1/1/xx	1/1/xx	Green	
Milestone Two	1/25/xx	1/25/xx	Green	
Milestone Three	2/15/xx	2/15/xx	Green	
Milestone Four	4/1/xx	4/1/xx	Green	

A third format includes financial information. This status report format describes the current state of the project in comparison to both the project plan and the project budget. Financial reporting can take many forms and be in various levels of detail. The minimum information is the total project budget and the monies spent to date. These can further be broken down into the capital and expense budgeted and used, along with comments and issues related to project finances.

Financial information can be added to any status report format. Below is an example.

Goals for this week	▪ Goal One	% Complete/Status
	▪ Goal Two	% Complete/Status
Goals for next week	▪ Goal One	
	▪ Goal Two	
Issues	▪ Issue One	
	▪ Issue Two	
Budget	Capital Budgeted:	Capital Used to Date:
	Expense Budgeted:	Expense Used to Date:
Comments		

The audience of the report drives the content of the status report. The primary recipient is the project sponsor, who may defer to the program manager or project leader. The status report should be crafted to meet the routine reporting needs of the audience.

The content should meet the needs and expectations of the report audience in a format that is easy to understand.

Signoff Document

The signoff document is the official acknowledgement of the completion of the project. It should be reviewed and approved by the same group that approved the charter document.

The signoff document should re-state the goals, completion criteria and success criteria as stated in the charter, along with any changes to those items. It should list the learnings from the project and allow each signor an opportunity to make comments.

This is an excellent opportunity for the project manager to conduct a "Satisfaction Survey" on the project. The manager can solicit opinions on the project process, documentation, communication, etc. from the team members, managers, stakeholders and sponsors. This information can then be used to refine the process for the next project.

Reporting

Communication about the project is a key element in effective project management within a corporate environment. Reports and documents are distributed to various areas within the company to provide information on the goals and status of the project.

Reporting within the project team is carried out in conjunction with the status meeting. The meeting summary, status report, issues list and project plan are distributed to the team members following the scheduled meeting.

Reporting outside of the team is established in the early meetings with the project sponsor. The project team may identify additional recipients of project reporting in the first meeting and as the project progresses. Additional recipients may include key stakeholders and managers of related or dependent projects .

Reporting generally flows up though a hierarchy with reduced detail at each level.

The project manager will produce a status report that is sent to the program manager on a pre-determined schedule. This status report will contain the information that the program manager has requested. Usually this is a general status and a listing of major issues. The program manager will in turn create a summary report on the program, which may or may not include the individual project reports.

The recipients of the reports drive their content. Key among these is the project sponsor. The sponsor will define the level of detail needed in reporting to them. This will in turn influence the detail in the reporting to other levels of management.

Summary

Below is a review of the documents associated with a project and how they fit together.

The **Charter** outlines the goals, scope, approach and other key information for the project.

The **Approach Document** details the tenants and methodology that the team will use in developing and implementing their plans

The **Meeting Summaries** describe the topics and results of project meetings.

The **Project Plan** outlines the specific tasks that must be completed to produce the project deliverables. It also details who is responsible for the tasks, how they are dependent upon each other and the project timeline.

The **Requirements Document** lists the specific items the design must accommodate.

The **Design Document** describes the target of the project and details how the requirements will be met.

The **Issues List** details the issues that the team has encountered as they execute the plan. It also lists who is responsible for resolving the issue, the time allotted to resolve the issue and the impacts of the resolution on the project plan.

The **Status Report** communicates the progress of the team in the execution of the plan and the overall health of the project.

The **Signoff Document** acknowledges that the project is complete.

CHAPTER FIVE

Managing A Project

Managing a Project

The previous four chapters have discussed the various aspects of managing projects. Chapter One discussed the process of project management. Chapter Two reviewed the individuals involved in the project team and their responsibilities. The Project Charter was discussed in Chapter Three. Chapter Four presented the various forms of documentation the project manager can use to communicate information about the project.

Tips on Meetings

Meetings are an essential part of managing any project. They can also be the greatest problem in managing a project. The ability to effectively facilitate meetings is one of the most important attributes a project manager can have. A well run meeting produces solid results and leaves the participants with a feeling that their time was well spent. Here are a few guidelines:

Hold meetings as scheduled

If a weekly meeting is scheduled, hold it weekly. Meetings that are canceled on a regular basis are not taken seriously by the participants. If a weekly meeting is cancelled every other week, it should be rescheduled as a bi-weekly meeting. The meeting schedule should fit the purpose of and demand for the meeting.

Make meetings meaningful

Do not have a meeting just because it is scheduled. If the time is not meaningful to the participants, review the purpose of the meeting to determine if it is necessary. If the meeting is necessary, review the schedule and approach to keep the participants engaged. The schedule can be adjusted if meetings are too frequent. If the meeting is too long it can be broken into two sessions. Asking the group what they think will make the time spent in the meeting more worth while. The responsibility of the project manager is to recognize the issue and bring it to the group's attention.

Have an agenda

Know what the desired outcome of the meeting is before scheduling it. Identify the topics to be discussed, the order and approximately how much time will be devoted to each. Announce the desired outcomes at the beginning of the meeting. It is helpful to publish the agenda before the meeting so the participants can arrive prepared to discuss the topics.

To create an agenda, list the goals of the meeting. Common goals are to inform the group, perform a demonstration or to make a decision. Under each goal, list the actions that group must take to reach the goal. Define how much time will be devoted to each of the actions and who will be leading the discussion. This will provide a rough draft of the agenda and the meeting timeline.

Prior to distributing the agenda, contact each of the individuals that should lead a discussion to make sure that they are aware of the topic they will be leading and are prepared to take part in the meeting.

Be the First to Come and the Last to Leave

Get to the meeting a little early. That demonstrates your commitment and assures participants that they are in the right place. Staying a few minutes after the meeting also demonstrates a commitment to the project. Rushing off after the meeting may make some participant uncomfortable.

Also, informal conversations after meeting often accomplish more then the meeting itself!

Send all of the Meeting Information in a Single Communication

The meeting notice or invitation should contain all of the information that is available for the meeting. The invitation should include the time, date, place, purpose and agenda or schedule. Reference aspects of the meeting that have yet to be determined. This will assure the invitees that these details are being addressed.

Re-confirm all meeting information in subsequent communications.

Look the Part

Have a professional appearance and dress appropriately for the group. Don't be casual if everyone else is formal; don't be formal if everyone else is casual. Whatever you wear it should be clean, pressed, fit properly and of a style appropriate for the environment.

Watch the Clock

Monitor the progress of the meeting in relation to the agenda. Don't wait until the end of the meeting to point out that the group is behind schedule. Ask the group if they want to continue a discussion that is using more than its allotted time. Make sure they understand that prolonging the conversation may limit their ability to cover the full agenda.

Take Care of the Logistical Details

Arrange for a room that is large enough to seat everyone comfortably. Make sure that everyone attending the meeting knows where and when the meeting is. Ensure that the necessary facilities and equipment are available. Arrange for a conference call if applicable and make sure that everyone has the call information. Confirm the details prior to the meeting. Arrive a little early to make sure that everything is arranged to your liking.

Ask Participants to Turn Cell Phones and Pagers Off (Or at least turn the ringers off)

This isn't just a matter of courtesy. The participants are in the meeting because their input is needed. Calls and pages divert attention away from the meeting, distract other participants and disrupt the flow of the meeting. Participants can retrieve pages and return calls after the meeting or during breaks. If phones and pagers cannot be turned off, they should be put into a "quiet" mode so they do not disturb other participants.

Ask Someone Else to Take Notes

It is quite difficult to facilitate a meeting and capture the discussion on paper at the same time. If possible, have a staff member or project coordinator take notes in the meeting. If this is not possible, ask a team member to provide a copy of their notes. If the facilitator documents the meeting, items should be noted on a white board or flip chart and transcribed during a break or after the meeting.

Stand Up!

Standing during a meeting signifies who is in charge. It also provides a better vantage point to view the group and their reactions.

Be Mobile

Walk around the room. Varying position in the room provides a gentle variety to the meeting environment that helps maintain team members' interest. Also, being mobile allows the facilitator to place himself or herself opposite the person speaking. This will bring the individuals between the facilitator and the speaker into the discussion.

Encourage discussion

Meetings are an exchange of ideas. Solicit opinions from participants on the topics as well as the management of the meeting.

Put people on the spot-gently

Some team members may be reluctant to voice concerns unless asked. Survey the group for body language that indicates questions or concerns. Ask those team members showing concern for their opinions on the topic.

Keep the group on subject

If the group is straying from the subject at hand, diplomatically bring them back to topic. For instance: "These are all good points, but remember that the goal of the meeting is to..." If the discussion has identified additional points, perhaps another meeting should be scheduled to address them.

Don't waste time speculating

If the expertise to resolve an issue is not present, do not spend a great deal of time speculating on possible solutions. Postpone the discussion until the proper resources can be brought in.

Face issues head on

Don't let issues linger. If the group is divided on a topic, ask them to voice their concerns. It is better to get things out and resolve them early then try to deal with them later.

Keep things light

No matter how serious the subject, an atmosphere of comfort and cooperation enhances the results of most meetings. People tend to be more cooperative when they are relaxed. Keeping a light, yet businesslike attitude in the meeting can be very helpful in gaining the cooperation of the team members. Also, attendance at meetings will be better if there is a high comfort level among the participants.

Ask, don't tell

Phrase your statements as questions. Say "Is this the direction we want the discussion to go?" instead of "This is not the direction the discussion should go." This will help maintain a relaxed atmosphere and solicit better cooperation. The members of the team usually have more knowledge of the subject matter. It is up to them to decide if the discussion is appropriate. It is the responsibility of the project manager to bring up the question.

Say "Thank You"

Thank participants for their input. Whether they have made a formal presentation or merely participated in a discussion. This will foster a higher level of participation from the group as a whole.

Be flexible

Don't become so entrenched in the agenda that the goal of the meeting gets lost. If the agenda isn't working, change it! Ask the group if they feel they are making progress. If not, try a different approach. The focus of the meeting is achieving the goals. It is much better to change the process and attain the goal than to maintain the process and miss the goal.

Learn to "Read the Room"

Pay attention to the behavior of the meeting participants. Be prepared to change the meeting format if participants seem distracted or uninterested. Keep mental notes of the agenda items that hold their interest or spark participation.

Check the phone

If there are meeting participants on a speakerphone, be sure to periodically ask them for comments. Participants on the phone my be difficult to hear or may be uncomfortable interrupting to make a comment.

When in doubt, ask the group

Ask the group their opinion about the approach to the meeting. The team members' time is valuable and they are the best judges of its use.

Don't be afraid to look foolish

Project managers are not required to have extensive knowledge on the project subject matter. By openly admitting this, the project manager can ask for explanations of topics that experts might consider common knowledge. It is the project manager's responsibility to ask the key questions that bring the issues to light and ensure that the entire group has a clear understanding of the situation. The project manager that doesn't complete the project on time is the real fool!

Resolve Conflicts

One of the purposes of a meeting is to bring differing views on a subject together and develop a unified plan. In these situations, conflicts arise that must be resolved.

It is important that the decision making process be established. *General Agreement* is the most common. General Agreement (Also known as *consensus*) is an opinion held by all or most of the team members. Those that are opposed are not fervent in their opposition and are willing to go along with the group. In most cases a *unanimous* decision is not necessary. A unanimous decision is reached through an actual vote with all members agreeing. Bringing a group to a unanimous decision can be time consuming and force team members to more entrenched in opinions and actually push the team farther from agreement. Unanimous decisions should be used when required by a documented meeting procedure.

The ultimate authority in the project is the sponsor. The sponsor has the ability to over ride any decision of the group by virtue of their position within the organization.

This should be a last resort. Forcing a decision on the group could undermine the spirit of cooperation within the group. The group must be a part of the decision process.

If the sponsor does exercise this authority, it is important that each opinion is voiced clearly and the decision is made openly.

If conflict persists on a particular point, the project manager may suggest any of the following actions:

- Make sure the topic of the conflict is pertinent to the goals of the project. If not, taking the time to bring the group to resolution is not necessary.

- Remind the group of the goal, scope and/or approach of the project that was agreed upon in the first meeting.
- Ask the group to play out a number of scenarios using the various ideas
- Refer the issue to the project sponsor, gaining commitment from the group to abide by the sponsor's decision.
- Postpone the decision until the issue can be researched or expert resources brought in.

Review deliverables at the end of the meeting

Remind the group of the deliverables that have been assigned to individuals in the meeting and when those deliverables are due.

What to bring

Copies of the materials for the meeting should be provided to all participants. The material should also be available to telephone participants. Documents from previous meetings should be available at all project meetings. These documents are useful references of previous work and include the project charter, plan, issue list and summaries of previous meetings. These should be available if needed. Multiple copies are not required.

These concepts apply regardless of the size or type of meeting being held.

Phase One—Getting Organized

Concept

The concept of a project can come from many sources. Wherever the concept originates, it must move up the organization to a level that has the authority to initiate it. This is usually where the sponsor is identified. In many organizations, a project is outlined and budgeted before a project manager is assigned. In any case, the project manager should meet with the sponsor to ensure that they have an understanding of the vision that the project should fulfill. This meeting will be very high level, with few details being addressed. The purpose is to reach a common understanding of the sponsor's goals and why the sponsor feels the project is important.

It is also important to discuss the project manager's approach with the sponsor. This serves to manage the sponsor's expectations and resolve any issues with the project management process before the project begins. This will also clarify the level of involvement the sponsor wants to have in the day to day operation of the project. The sponsor's reporting expectations can also be defined.

Assembling a Team

The project sponsor can assist in identifying the key members of the project team. There should be at least one representative of each organizational area that will be required to contribute to the project. Major stakeholders may also be included. Project team members should have a level of expertise that allows them to act as subject matter experts and have sufficient authority to bring in additional resources as necessary. They must also be able to devote the proper time to the project. The sponsor may contact their peers in the various areas to request resources be assigned to the project.

The project manager should contact the team members individually and provide some background into the project. This will aid in securing the team member's commitment to the project and prepare the team for the first meeting.

First Meeting

With a clear vision of the concept and the key team members identified and committed, the team should be assembled for their first meeting. The goals of the first meeting include:

- Create a common understanding of the goals of the project
- Develop a Project Charter
- Establish roles and responsibilities of team members
- Develop a Project Plan

- Establish future meeting schedule
- Establish reporting and documentation expectations
- Identify additional resources that should be added to the team.

The first meeting (also known as the kickoff, launch, organizational, etc.) can last a few hours or several days. The complexity of some projects may require that the first meeting be divided into two or more sessions. Defining the many aspects of a complex project can be very taxing on the participants and it is important that the group stay focused though the entire process.

The first meeting sets the tone and the pace for the entire project. The Project Charter documents the goals and processes for the project. The Project Plan establishes the project tasks and timeline. The entire team should attend the first meeting.

The sponsor and project manager should meet to establish the agenda for the first meeting and to make sure they are in agreement on the organization of the meeting.

The team should be assembled in one location if possible. First meetings via telephone or videoconference generally are less effective. Some type of team-building exercise is also beneficial as this may be the only time that everyone associated with the project is assembled.

The sponsor should open the meeting with remarks on the events that brought this project into being. The sponsor should share their vision of the results of the project and the capabilities it will produce. The sponsor's remarks should be followed by an introduction by the project manager. The project manager's remarks should include comments on their project philosophy and logistics of the first meeting.

An introduction of the attendees should be included in either the sponsor's comments or the project manager's comments. The goal of the introduction is to identify the members of the team and to begin creating an atmosphere of comfort and cooperation between individuals and areas that may not have worked together before. In most cases it is best to have the team members introduce themselves. This allows the team to match a face with a voice. It is also a good idea to relax the group by asking an out-of-the-ordinary question during the introductions. For example, team members might be asked to give their name, the area they represent and to tell the group what their favorite color is and why. Another good question is to have the meeting participants identify their favorite movie. This not only helps the team to get to know each other, but the introductions will hold the groups interest and will most likely spawn some off-line conversations.

Create the Project Charter

With the opening remarks and introductions complete, the Project Charter should be addressed. As discussed in Chapter 3, the project charter includes these items:

    Goal Statement
    Executive Summary
    Approach
    Scope
    Project Justification
    Constraints
    Organization
    Completion Criteria
    Success Criteria
    Timeline/Schedule
    Assumptions & Dependencies
    Impacts
    Change Control Process

The first meeting should address all of these topics with few exceptions. While the charter itself is vital to the success of the project, the processed used to create the document is of equal importance. The team must create the charter as a group. Participation in decisions on goals, approach and deliverables instills a sense of commitment in team members. Creation of the charter also brings out initial issues and questions within the team that can be resolved in the session, thereby clarifying many aspects of the project. Creating the charter as a group also ensures that all members of the team are aware of the contents of the charter. This establishes an understanding of what the project is trying to accomplish, why it is important and defines each team member's role.

The executive summary can be created after the meeting using information from other sections of the charter and general background knowledge. The project manager usually drafts this for the approval of the sponsor and team members.

The project justification may have been created prior to the first meeting. An overview of the justification would be of interest to the team and should be presented. The team may be able to identify additional benefits or costs that may make the justification more accurate.

The charter document should be created by the group through a *facilitated session*. The project manager should lead the group through discussions to determine the content of the charter. There may be some conflict within the group in this process. It is much better to identify and resolve this conflict in the first meeting than have it surface during the project execution. Once the charter is accepted by the group it is difficult to change, so it must be approved by the entire team.

Goals

Defining the goal of the project can be the most time consuming aspect of the entire first meeting. In many cases the team members will have very different ideas as to what the project is all about. The project sponsor may have a clear vision, but the team must develop the specific goals with guidance from the sponsor and project manager. Team participation in establishing the specific goals will generate a stronger commitment to the goals. It also allows the experts in the field to contribute to the process. This may also uncover aspects of the environment that the sponsor and project manager had not considered in their previous meetings.

The goal statement must be carefully crafted to reflect the true intent of the project. Once finalized, it should be posted it in the meeting room. Refer to the goal often when developing the other sections of the charter and other documents for the project. When the group digresses into discussions that are not related to the goal, remind them gently using the goal statement. Something like "Is this conversation leading us closer to our goal?". The group can then decide if they want to continue or move on to another topic.

Approach

Developing a detailed Approach may be beyond the scope of the first meeting. On larger projects the approach may be limited to a high-level projection of the tenets that the team will adhere to when developing their plans. In this case a detailed approach document would be published at a later date.

Scope

The definition of the project scope is key to managing the expectations of the stakeholders. The team must establish the boundaries of the project. Items that are within scope and out of scope are equally important.

Start with the basics. What systems, locations, products, etc. are involved? If portions of these items are involved, list them separately. The list should be detailed enough to be accurate, but not so detailed that it cannot be understood. For example:

> In Scope
>
> - All offices in North Carolina
> - All offices in South Carolina except #23 & #24
> - Offices #7 and #10 in Virginia

The purpose of listing the items that are out of scope is to avoid confusion on what may be assumed to be within scope but in fact is not. A reasonable level of detail must be maintained. It isn't reasonable to list ALL of the items that are not within the scope of a project (That would be quite a list!) The items listed as "out of scope" should be limited to those that are related to the project but not covered by it. When in doubt, include the item. If anyone on the team feels that there could be confusion, there will certainly be confusion out of the team. It is better to have too much detail than not enough.

Project Justification

As discussed earlier, the project justification may have been created as a separate exercise prior to the first meeting. If so, the sponsor or project manager should present an overview of the justification to give the team an idea of the impact they are having on the organization.

The project justification should be discussed with the project team. Members of the team may have additional input into the costs and benefits of the project. These should be noted, discussed and investigated. The group may bring to light aspects of the justification that had not previously been considered.

The project justification may be impacted by the definition of scope. The justification should be reviewed after the charter has been finalized.

Constraints

List any limits on the project. For example: "All renovation to the school building must be complete before the first day of class".

Organization

Identify the individuals that are filling key roles and clearly define their responsibilities. Resolve any overlap or gaps in these roles and responsibilities. It is also important to identify who will sign off on the project when complete. This is usually the sponsor, program manager and selected stakeholders.

Refer to the individuals by their title within the project rather than by name. Use "The project sponsor" rather than "Mr. Johnson". The individual filling a particular role may change during the course of a project.

Using titles will eliminate the need of re-drafting the charter with every change in personnel.

Completion Criteria

Ask the group to identify the key deliverables that will signify the completion of the project. These deliverables must be within the scope of the project that the group agreed upon. Deliverables that are out-of-scope should be omitted.

Success Criteria

Ask the group to identify the measurements that will denote the success of the project. The Project Justification may be helpful in this section. Elements listed in the success criteria must be easily measured in both the current and target environments. Items such as production time, service calls, downtime, etc. can be used only if the information is readily available. Criteria that are based on a measure that does not exist or is difficult to obtain should not be used.

The Success Criteria is often displayed as a table that demonstrates the difference between the current and target environments. It may be helpful to develop this table with the group.

Current Environment Measurements	Target Environment Measurements
(1) 100	(1) 150
(2) 3 Days	(2) 2 Days

Timeline/Schedule

The timeline presented in the charter is very high level. It includes only a few milestones to describe the intended progress. It can include only the project phases. A detailed timeline will be developed with the Project Plan.

Milestone	Completion Date
Establish Requirements	02/01/XX
Complete Design	03/01/XX
Build	5/01/XX
Implement	6/01/XX

Assumptions & Dependencies

Ask the group to list the assumptions they used in defining the previous items and any other areas of the organization that the project is dependent upon. Also list the impacts associated with the failure of the assumptions and dependencies.

Impacts

Ask the group to identify how this project will impact other areas of the organization.

Change Control Process

Establish the process for changes to the project. This should include criteria for the types of changes that must be approved, who should approve them and who should be notified.

Sample Text:

The Project Sponsor must approve changes to the scope, timeline and/or deliverables. Proposed changes must be presented in writing to the sponsor with documentation of the ramifications of the change. Criteria for changes that must be approved are as follows:

- Changes that delay the project one week or more from the original delivery date
- Changes that increase the budget more than 10% above the approved estimate
- Any change to project deliverables

In this example the charter has provided the team with a one-week time cushion, a 10% budget cushion and no cushion on deliverables.

Develop a Project Plan

After the charter has been agreed upon, a plan to reach the goals should be developed. The Project Plan outlines the specific tasks required to complete the project. There are two types of project plans: the High Level Plan and the Detail Plan.

The high level plan summarizes tasks to create the project timeline. The detail plan breaks the summary tasks into line items. The timeline of the summary plan may be several weeks or months. It is difficult to make detailed plans months in advance of the actual event. Even if it were easy to plan that far in advance, the tasks would most likely change in the interim.

The high level plan should be created at the first meeting. It will be difficult to anticipate the tasks necessary to implement the design if the design has not yet been completed. The high-level plan will establish the estimated timeline and provide a guide for the detailed plans. The planning horizon for the detailed plan should be 3-4 weeks and can be created in subsequent team meetings.

As with the charter, it is important that the team develop the high-level project plan as a group. This will assist in making sure the plan is realistic and includes all necessary aspects of the project. Developing the project as a group also guarantees that each team member understands their commitments.

It is crucial that the plan be realistic. The time it will take to complete a task must be accurate. The timeline presented in the plan must be a true estimate of the actual time it will take to complete the project. This is a key to managing expectations. Stakeholders will expect delivery in the time set forth in the charter. If the timeline is not realistic, the project is sure to miss delivery. The group should be asked periodically if the timelines are reasonable.

A good check for the thoroughness of the plan is to identify the deliverables listed in the Completion Criteria section of the Charter. All deliverables should be accounted for as the plan develops. If the group is reluctant to include a deliverable in the project plan, they should be questioned as to whether or not the deliverable should be in the Charter. If it's in the Charter, it must be in the plan.

After the plan is complete, review the Assumptions & Dependencies section of the Charter with the group. If the group feels it is appropriate, create contingency plans for the failure of one of these items.

The subject matter experts on the project team should be able to provide the information necessary to develop the plan. The project manager's responsibility is to see that the plan is organized and complete. Each of the process steps discussed in Charter One should be accounted for. Concept, Budget, Approach and Scope have been accounted for in the Charter Document. The Project Plan will cover Requirements, Design, Build and Implement.

The steps of the project plan are call *tasks.* Each task has a *duration,* the time it takes to complete a task. Some tasks have *dependencies.* That is, the task cannot be started or be completed until another task has started or is completed. A *predecessor* is a task that another is dependent upon. *Resources* are assigned to tasks. A resource is the individual responsible for completion of the task. A single resource should be made responsible for each task. The assigned resource may bring others to the task, but the resource assigned is ultimately responsible for completion.

The project plan must be limited to those tasks that are essential to achieving the project goals. This helps to simplify the plan. More importantly, if the task is not essential to achieving the project goals, it is out of the project scope and the team should not devote resources to it.

Each task listed in the plan is an action that must be completed by the resource. Therefore, the description of a task should include a verb. A task is an action. A task is to *complete, build, design, research, present, construct, assemble, deliver, etc.*

There are several approaches to creating a project plan. This text will discuss three successful approaches.

The "Post-It Note" Game

In this approach, the team members are asked to list all of the tasks involved in completing the project deliverables, the task's duration and who should complete the task. The team needn't be concerned about the order of the tasks at this point. The goal is to identify the tasks. The facilitator writes descriptions of the tasks on large post-it notes, one task per note. These notes are hung on a wall of the meeting room.

When all of the tasks have been identified, ask the team to arrange the notes on the wall form a timeline for the project. The facilitator should arrange the notes under the direction of the team. Concurrent tasks are placed above and below each other on the wall. Dependent tasks are placed to the right of their predecessors. For clarity, predecessors may be written on the note with the task. As the notes are arranged on the wall, lines of tasks will begin to form. The lines cross at the point where they are dependent upon each other. As the game continues, tasks can be added, modified or deleted as the group decides.

Example of the Post-It Note Game

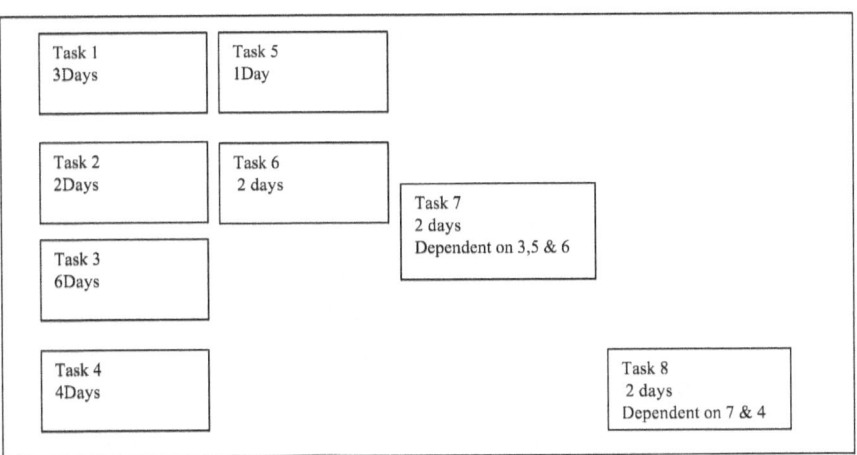

Tasks 1,2,3 and 4 are concurrent tasks. They can be completed simultaneously and are not dependent upon each other. Task 5 cannot be started until task 1 is complete (Task 5 is dependent upon task 1) Task 6 is dependent upon task 2. Tasks 5 and 6 are concurrent. Task 7 is dependent upon tasks 3, 5 and 6. Task 8 is dependent upon tasks 7 and 4. Task 8 is the final deliverable of the project.

Determining Timelines

A series of tasks that form a continuous line from the beginning of the project to the end is known as a *path*. In the previous example, tasks 2, 6, 7 and 8 form a path. The *timeline* is the schedule created by the individual durations in the path. The sum of the durations of the tasks in the path is the *total duration*. The largest total duration is the duration of the project.

The timelines of our example are:

Path	Timeline	Total Duration
1,5,7,8	3+1+2+2	8 Days
2,6,7,8	2+2+2+2	8 Days
3,7,8	6+2+2	10 Days
4,8	4+2	8 Days

The longest timeline is "3,7,8" with a duration of 10 days. The timeline that determines the project duration is referred to as the *critical path*. This path is considered critical because any delays in the tasks that are on this path will delay the final delivery date.

The other timelines have 2 days of *lag time*. Lag time is the difference between the timeline and the critical path. These tasks may be delayed up to the amount of lag time without impacting the overall project

Most project management software packages will track dependencies, calculate timelines and identify the critical path. Tasks are entered into the software with their durations and dependencies noted. The software uses this information to determine the project timeline.

A Variation on the Post-It Note Game

A variation on the Post-It Note Game is to divide the project into the phases that the plan will cover. A common phased structure is the four phases listed in Chapter One: Requirements, Design, Build and

Implement. Instead of assembling the entire plan in a single effort, conduct the process in four phases. First, define the tasks and timeline for the Requirements. Then, after documenting the results, remove the notes and define the tasks for the Design phase. Repeat the process for the Build and Implement phases.

The Phased Approach

Another popular method to develop a project plan is to use an erasable board to document the tasks. Ask the group to list the high level phases of the project. Write these across the top of the board. Under each high level task, document the items that need to be completed as part of that task, along with the time requirements, dependencies and the responsible resource.

Example of the phases of changing a flat tire. Total Time: 13 minutes

Jack up the car	Remove Flat Tire	Install Spare Tire	Remove the Jack	Clean Up
Open Truck Remove Jack Remove Spare Tire Place under car Raise car	Remove lug nuts Remove tire	Place spare tire on lugs Replace lug nuts	Lower the car Remove the jack	Place jack in trunk Place flat tire in trunk Close trunk
Time: 5 Minutes	Time: 2 Minutes	Time: 2 Minutes	Time: 2 Minutes	Time: 2 Minutes

The phased approach works well with projects that are linear in nature. That is, they follow a clean progression from one task to another with few concurrent tasks. The Post-it Note Game work well for projects that have a number of concurrent tasks.

With identification of tasks complete, the information can be assembled into a formal project plan.

Other Topics for the First Meeting

Establish the Meeting & Reporting Schedules

As part of the first meeting, the team must establish how often to meet, how long these meetings will last and how they will be conducted (in person, conference call or videoconference). The group should also establish the distribution list and schedule for status reports, issue lists and updated project plans. Distribution of these documents is generally on the same schedule as the status meeting. The team should also identify who should sign off on the completed project.

Define Project Status

The team should also define the status reporting structure as discussed in Chapter 4 (Red/Yellow/Green etc) and the criteria for each status. As an example, the team may designate that the "Green" status indicates that all tasks are being completed within established tolerances. "Yellow" will signify that issues have delayed the tasks currently due, but the team feels they can make up the time and deliver on time and within budget. "Red" will indicate that the project will not meet its objective on time. The Change Management process described in the charter can then be used to alter the project to fit the new environment.

Establish the Project "Drivers"

The "Drivers" of a project are the Budget, Deliverables and the Timeline. The team should establish a hierarchy of these drivers. If an issue places the team in a situation where it must choose between increasing the budget or missing the timeline, which is the appropriate action? By establishing the hierarchy at the first meeting, the team will know in advance the guidelines for making these recommendations. Definition of the "Drivers" will also provide guidelines for the issues that must pass through the Change Control process described in the Charter. The Constraints listed on the charter will also contribute to the hierarchy of drivers.

Follow-up to the First Meeting

The focus of the first meeting is organization. At the meeting the group develops a charter, agrees to roles and responsibilities, creates a high-level project plan and establishes a schedule for future meetings and communication. A summary of the meeting should be produced and distributed to the attendees as soon after the meeting as possible. The summary should include a discussion of the decisions made and copies of the charter document and project plan.

The team should re-convene as agreed to review the project documents prior to distribution. With the final versions of the documents agreed upon, they may be distributed to all interested parties.

Phase Two—Execution

With the charter created and the project plan in place, the project team can begin the process of executing the tasks listed on the plan. The project manager must monitor the progress against the timeline, report on the progress and see that issues are identified and resolved.

Keeping a Project on Schedule

The best way to keep a project on schedule is to start with a *realistic* schedule. As discussed earlier, the timeline must reflect what can reasonably be accomplished.

A key to keeping projects on schedule is to lead by example. The project manager must complete deliverables on time. If project managers do not complete items as assigned, they cannot expect team members to. A project manager's deliverables may include the creation of status reports, meeting summaries, draft documents, and other related activities. These must be delivered as promised.

Delays will threaten most projects. These are monitored through the issue list and communicated through the status reports. The following actions can help to mitigate issues that threaten the project:

- Clearly identify the issue and how the resolution impacts the timeline.

A clear picture of the situation will allow the team to identify alternatives for resolving the issue.

- Review the Project Plan to clearly define the impact on the project delivery date

  Add the tasks to the plan to determine how they impact other deliverables. Determine if the additional tasks impact the project's critical path.

- Is the delay significant enough that the team feels it must be addressed?

  If the delay does not impact the final delivery date, the sponsor should be informed and the situation communicated in the status report.

- Develop alternatives

  Ask the team to brainstorm on ways to complete the project on time in spite of the delay. The team should recommend a course of action to the sponsor with details of the impacts of the resolution.

- Review the task dependencies

  Can tasks be altered to minimize the impact of the delay? Can dependent tasks become concurrent tasks? Can any work be done on dependent tasks before the issue is resolved?

- Can additional resources be used to speed up the resolution?
- Can the project get back on schedule with overtime?
- Can the cause of the delay be omitted or bypassed?

After developing alternatives, they should be reviewed according to the hierarchy of "Drivers" established at the first meeting. Most of the alternatives to bring the project on schedule will impact either the budget or the deliverables.

For example:

- If additional resources or overtime will resolve the issue without impacting the timeline, the project budget may be impacted.
- Altering the relationships between the tasks (Dependencies) may impact the functionality of the deliverables.

- Omitting or bypassing the cause of the issue may impact the deliverables.

By establishing the priority of budget, timeline and deliverables, the team can evaluate the alternatives and make recommendations to the project sponsor.

Dealing with Delays

If a delay is not avoidable, the change control process should be implemented to inform the appropriate areas. A revised timeline must be developed and approved.

Delays are not necessarily a poor reflection on the project manager or the project team. The project manager and team have done their jobs if they have identified the threat, developed alternatives, planned their actions and communicated promptly.

Team Meetings

Team meetings are divided into two categories: Status Meetings and Working Meetings

Status Meetings

Status meeting are held periodically on a regular, pre-set schedule. All members of the project team should attend. The purpose of the status meeting is to:

- Identify tasks that have recently been completed
- Make detailed plans for upcoming tasks (3-4 future meetings)
- Identify and assign issues that have been discovered
- Review the status of open issues
- Provide a forum for the discussion between team members
- Provide general information to the project team

The status meetings will see the team through the Requirements, Design, Build and Implement phases. While these phases may overlap, the team should always be aware of their status in relation to their plan.

Sample Status Meeting Agenda:

Opening Remarks

Review of Project Plan
Overall Status
Past Due Items
Current Items
Future Items
New Items

Review of Issues List
Past Due Issues
Current Issues
Future Issues
New Issues

Other News/Discussion/Questions

Review of Deliverables from this Meeting

Notes on future meetings
Time/Location/Subjects

Status meetings should be held to less than one hour. If the meeting is consistently over one hour, the group should be asked if they are comfortable devoting that amount of time to the status. If not, the format or schedule can be changed to make the meeting more efficient.

Issue Resolution

The status meeting is a forum to identify issues; it is not a forum to resolve issues. After an issue is identified, an individual will be assigned to the issue and this information logged into the Issues List. The responsible person will organize the necessary resources to resolve the issue and report the findings to the group. It is important that a single individual be named as responsible for the issue. Divided responsibility usually leads to confusion as to who must actually carry out the tasks. A single individual responsible for the issue eliminates this confusion.

Another key factor in issue resolution is to define the date that the resolution is due. Issues cannot be allowed to linger unresolved. The anticipated resolution date should be defined in the status meeting and referred to in subsequent meetings. These gentle reminders will help keep the project on schedule. A good portion of the status meeting will be devoted to discussion of the Issues List. There should be no discussion of closed issues. Discussion of open issues that are not due should be limited to a reminder of the due date. Team members that are presenting resolutions should be given sufficient time to cover their topic and field questions.

When the resolution of an issue has been identified and agreed upon, the issue is closed. The tasks necessary to resolve the issue are added to the project plan and the ramifications of the additional tasks is determined. If the addition of the tasks impacts the timeline, budget or deliverables, refer to the "Keeping A Project on Schedule" suggestions discussed earlier in this chapter.

Reporting on the project should not be so time consuming that it interferes with the execution of the project. A status meeting is a checkpoint on progress against the project plan. It should be short, to the point and organized. The project manager should facilitate the meeting and ask the appropriate team members to take responsibility for tasks and issues. If an involved discussion develops, the project manager should suggest that a separate meeting be scheduled to address the topic.

Working Meetings

These are meetings that are scheduled to accomplish a specific item on the project plan. These are not generally regular, weekly meetings. They are scheduled as needed and vary in length and format. They may be facilitated by the project manager or a team member, though the project manager should attend as many as possible. A meeting to resolve an issue is a good example of a working meeting.

Adjustments to the Project Plan

As the tasks listed on the project plan are completed, the team may develop a better way to fulfill the design. As the team becomes more familiar with the details of the initiative, they may uncover a more suitable approach. It is not uncommon for an innovative team to decide that the project plan should take a new direction. It is the project manager's responsibility to ensure that the group understands all of the ramifications of such a change. These ramifications may include re-work of completed tasks, obsolescence of equipment or facilities, a change in the deliverables or an impact on the budget and/or timeline. Any radical change to the project plan, even if the ramifications are minor, should be approved by the sponsor in accordance with the change control process.

Establishing the Requirements-"What"

The project requirements establish *what* specific functionality will be delivered by the project. They are based on the Project Goals, Completion Criteria and Success Criteria described in the Charter. The requirements are used to develop the design of the target environment for the project.

A number of groups take part in developing the requirements. Among these are the stakeholders and the area responsible for implementation. Other areas take part as designated in the Project Plan.

Requirements can be described as the answers to a series of questions. The questions vary with the project, but can be summed up as:

- What size?
- How many?
- How much?
- How fast?
- What kind?

Requirements detail what must be delivered to accomplish the goals of the project. The requirements must be detailed enough to give the designers a clear understanding of what is needed without needlessly limiting their flexibility. An aspect of the desired functionality that is not addressed will be left to the discretion of the designer.

Requirements are divided into two types: *functional* requirements and *specific* requirements.

Functional requirements describe what the design should do, without specifying how it is to be done. These describe the end result, without specifying the method. "The process must deliver 100 assembled units per hour" is an example. This statement does not specify how the units are to be assembled. The method of assembly is left to the designers.

Specific requirements provide more detail to the designers. The company may be contractually obligated to a specific process or have infrastructure that limits the design. "Existing facilities will be modified to increase production to 100 assembled units per hour" is an example. This statement directs the design team to limit their efforts to existing facilities.

A typical requirements document will contain both functional and specific requirements. An explanation should be attached to specific a requirement that explains why they are restricted. If the group cannot justify a specific requirement, the item should be re-phrased to remove the restriction.

A list of individuals that can be contacted with questions about the requirements should be supplied to the design team.

Gathering Requirements

The term used to describe the process of documenting the project requirements is *gathering*. The project team must gather the requirements from various groups and distill them into a single document. There are often conflicts and contradictions within the requirements that must be resolved. A single, clear and thorough set of requirements must be presented to the design team.

No matter what method is used to gather the requirements, the design team should be consulted before the process begins. The designers should identify any specific questions that the requirements must answer.

A common method of requirements gathering is to forward a questionnaire to the stakeholders. The questionnaire must be thorough enough to gather the information in sufficient detail for the design team. The design team should participate in developing the questionnaire.

After the questionnaire is returned, the individual responding to the questionnaire should be contacted and their responses verified and any questions addressed. Documents from various areas can then be compared to find conflicts. The areas involved in the conflicts can be contacted to seek resolution.

Gathering requirements by questionnaire appears on the surface as a quick way to accomplish the task. However, only in very simple projects can this be done effectively. With even a low level of complexity the questionnaire method becomes very cumbersome with follow-up and conflict resolution.

In some cases, the team may assemble all of the contributing groups to complete the requirements in a combined session. In other cases, it may be appropriate to meet with the groups individually and assemble the requirements after all of the sessions are complete.

The combined session can be the most expedient way to develop requirements. With all of the groups represented, conflicts and overlaps can be resolved during the sessions and the final product reviewed by all parties.

Individual sessions with each group are a viable alternative if a combined session is not practical. Individual sessions allow an in-depth and focused view of the group's needs. If separate sessions are used, all parties must review the assembled requirements and discrepancies resolved before the document is finalized.

It may be appropriate to distribute a questionnaire prior to the requirements sessions. The questions will prepare the groups for the sessions. The answers will provide the project team with information that will help structure the requirements sessions and get a head start on documenting the requirements.

At the end of each requirement session, the group should critique the requirement process. Both positive and negative comments should be solicited. The participants are an excellent source of suggestions to improve the process.

The process to define requirements is the same whether meeting in a large or small group. The participants should describe the function of the areas they represent. These should be posted where all participants can see them. The group should then describe the processes and activities that are needed to complete this function in the new environment. As each process or activity is identified, the group should phrase it as a requirement. Completing the requirements in a table is helpful.

Process	Function	Requirement	Notes
Security	External Surveillance	The security team must be able to observe the entire property continuously	
Security	Premises	Electronic alarms must be installed on all entrances and ground floor windows	Regulations specifically require electronic alarms on all entrances and ground floor windows

This format can also be used to create the requirements document. The final version of the requirements document should include a list of the individual requirements and the function that is supported. Note that in this example the first requirement is functional in that it indicates that the security team must observe, but does not specify how. The second requirement is specific in that it indicates that electronic alarms must be used.

Developing the Design-"How"

The design is the target environment of the project. The design is based on the requirements that are contained in the Requirements Document and limited by the constraints defined in the Charter. The requirements define *what* is needed and the design defines *how* the requirements will be met.

The design team is a group within the project team that has the technical expertise to carry out the design process. The project manager may not play an active roll in the design process, other than to monitor the progress. The major responsibility of the project manager is to ensure that the design satisfies the requirements as specified by the stakeholders. In cases where the requirements cannot be fulfilled, alternatives should be identified.

A good exercise to establish what the design encompasses is to add a column to the table used to develop the requirements. This column will explain how the design fulfills the requirement.

Process	Function	Requirement	Notes	Design
Security	Exterior Surveillance	The security team must be able to observe the entire property continuously		2 surveillance cameras installed on all corners of the building exterior, capturing 100% of grounds around facility
Security	Premises	Electronic alarms must be installed on all entrances and ground floor windows	Regulations specifically require electronic alarms on all entrances and ground floor windows	Electronic alarms installed in all exterior doors and ground floor windows

The design team may choose to present alternatives to the stakeholders. This can be carried out through individuals listed as contacts or in a formal presentation to a group of stakeholders. The design team should contact the project manager to make the necessary arrangements.

When the design is complete, the design team should present it to the project team to demonstrate how the design fulfills the requirements. The project sponsor and selected stakeholders may also want to attend the presentation.

Build

The "Build" phase delivers the design into production. This is where the requirements and the design become a reality. This is also where the project plan undergoes the greatest amount of stress.

Details of the build phase can be difficult to anticipate early in the project. Some aspects of the plan may have changed since the high-level plan was created in the first meeting. An additional session to create the plan for the Build and Implementation phases may be appropriate. The change management process must be implemented if the revised plan impacts the original specifications established in the charter.

Testing and training are key points that are often overlooked in the build phase. The project manager should make sure that all of the appropriate topics are addressed in the plan.

Status meetings are used to monitor progress and identify issues.

Implement

After the solution has been built and properly tested, the implementation phase moves the changes created by the project into production. This may be a hard switch, a transition or in phases. The plan should detail what the steps are to move from the current environment to the target environment. Through the status and working meetings, the project manager can monitor the progress through implementation.

Signoff

The project team should be assembled for a debriefing after the project is complete. The purpose of the debrief is to gather the team's comments on the project and the project process. This is an excellent opportunity to critique the process and make improvements. This will also assist the project manager in preparing the signoff document.

The project manager distributes the signoff document to the sponsor, program manager and anyone else identified in the by the team at the first meeting. The signoff document contains several elements taken directly from the charter. These include the goals, completion criteria and success criteria. The document should include the project manager's comments on the team's success in delivering these items.

In most cases the project manager will not be able to address the success criteria. Some success criteria may not be measurable for some time after the project is completed. The signoff document should reference these items and explain when results will be available.

The signoff document should also contain the project manager's comments on the overall performance of the project team and the project process. The recipients of the signoff document should review and add their comments.

Summary

The steps in managing an initiative include:

Phase One-Organization

- Meet with the sponsor
  - Clearly define the sponsor's vision
  - Establish the project process
  - Define the sponsor's role
  - Clarify the project reporting requirements
- Assemble the team
  - Identify the subject areas involved
  - Obtain commitment from each area, with assistance from the sponsor
- Hold the first meeting
  - Create a common understanding of the goals of the project
  - Develop a Project Charter
  - Establish roles and responsibilities
  - Develop a Project Plan
  - Establish future meeting schedule
  - Establish reporting and documentation expectations

- Identify additional resources that should be added to the team

Phase Two-Execution

- Status
- Issues
- Reporting/Distribution
- Requirements
- Design
- Build
- Implement
- Signoff/Debrief

This process could take days, weeks, months or even years to complete. It is key to remain focused on the goals of the project and be flexible in the implementation. The team must play an active roll in developing deliverables and plans. The stakeholders must be involved in the development of the requirements and review the functionality provided by the design.

A very important aspect of successful project management is to maintain *balance.* The process is important, but cannot interfere with the objective. Flexibility is important, but the theme of the process must be held firm. Balance between flexibility and the process must be maintained. The goal of the project manager is to bring the team to the successful completion of the project. To do so may require some adjustments to the process used. Occasionally, project managers must be creative in their approach. A project manager cannot become so entrenched in the process that they lose sight of the purpose of project management—to complete projects.

The ultimate measurement of a project's success is the achievement of the project goals. The ultimate measurement of a project manager's success is the ability to complete the project deliverables on time and on budget, regardless of the process used.

Appendices

Sample Documents

The following documents are sample documentation of a typical project. These documents describe the construction of a home for a fictional family. The contents of these documents are intended to be examples of the type of information that various documents should contain. These documents are not intended to be a realistic description of the construction of a home.

Project Charter Document
The Jackson Home
January 1, XXXX

Contents

Goal Statement

To design and construct a residence for the Jackson family

Executive Summary

The Jackson family has been residing in their current home for approximately five years. The home was purchased when the Jacksons relocated as a result of a job change and was intended as a temporary residence. The Jacksons have added a child to their family since moving into their current home. Their other children will soon be entering school.

The current residence has several functional inadequacies that have prompted the Jacksons to investigate alternatives. Among these factors are:

- Capacity: The current residence has three bedrooms. The Jackson's now have three children and the home cannot accommodate them comfortably. The kitchen area is too small for current demands and the current residence has a single-car garage.
- Location: The current residence is a lengthy bus ride from the school

The popularity of homes in the area has limited the opportunities to purchase an existing home. In this light, the Jacksons have opted to build.

Approach

The approach to the project will include the selection of a builder followed by the selection of the building site. The quality of construction is a key element of the project. Therefore, selection of a quality builder of utmost importance. A location will be selected with the assistance of the builder.

With the building and location established, requirements for the design will be gathered and delivered to the design team. Construction will begin when the design has been approved.

Scope

In Scope

- Selection of a builder
- Selection of a location
- Securing of permits

- Defining requirements of the design
- Designing the structure
- Designing the landscaping
- Construction of the home and improvements to the lot.
    - Excavating
    - Masonry/Concrete Work
    - Foundation
    - Driveway
    - Façade
    - Sidewalks (including street sidewalk)
    - Fireplace (s)
- Carpentry
- Electrical
- Plumbing
- Heating/Air Conditioning
- Painting
- Floor Coverings
- Window Treatments
- Landscaping
- Utilities
    - Installation of gas lines
    - Installation of electrical
    - Installation of telephone lines
    - Installation of Cable Television lines

Out of Scope
- Improvements to streets and bridges
- Landscaping beyond property boundaries
- Installation of utilities beyond local hookups

- Moving the family's belongings into the home

Project Justification
Non-Financial Benefits

- Increased living space
- Shorter distance to school
- Updated appliances
- Updated heating and air conditioning
- Larger garage
- Larger yard

Financial Benefits*

- Reduced utility payments through more efficient heating and air conditioning
- Reduced fuel expense through shorter distance to work and school

*This text is presented for the sake of example. Anyone that has ever built a home knows that there is rarely a financial justification.

Constraints

The home must be ready for occupancy two weeks prior to the first day of the school year. (on or before August 15)

Organization

Project Sponsor: The Jackson Family
Responsibilities:

- Assist in identifying and securing team members
- Assist in the resolution of issues
- Secure project funding
- Approve project goals and deliverables
- Review project status
- Approve changes to the project

• Approve project completion (Signoff)

Project Manager: To Be Decided

Responsibilities:

- Identify/recommend potential team members
- Create and distribute project documents
- Coordinate and facilitate project meetings
- Coordinate activities of project team members
- Assign tasks and issues to the project team members
- Resolve issues and obtain decisions as needed to ensure successful completion of the project
- Review deliverables as completed
- Manage, control and report on project progress

Completion Criteria

This project will be considered complete when the following deliverables are completed:

- The residence is ready for occupancy in compliance with all applicable laws and regulations
- Construction is complete as specified in the design
- Landscaping is completed as specified in the design
- All remnants of construction (tools, scrap materials, signs, etc) have been removed from the property.

Success Criteria

Project success will be determined by the following factors:

Measure	Current Environment	Target Environment
Number of Bedrooms	3	4
Distance to School	2 Miles	1/4 Mile
Size of Garage	1 Car	2 Car
Size of lot	1/4 acre	1/2 Acre

Timeline/Schedule

Milestone	Delivery Date
Builder Selected	2/1
Requirements Defined	3/1
Location Selected	3/15
Design Finalized	4/17
Construction Begins	4/25
Foundation Complete	5/16
Framing Complete	6/27
Drywalling Complete	7/31
Construction Complete	8/11
Occupancy	8/15

Assumptions & Dependencies

Assumptions/Dependencies	Impacts
Weather does not present any unusual delays	Construction will be delayed by weather
Street improvements will be completed prior to 7/1	Street improvements will be delayed, thus delaying construction
Utility hookups will be available on site on or before 5/15	Utility hookups will not be available prior to the beginning of construction, causing delays to the timeline
The proper materials will be available	Materials will be unavailable or delayed, thus delaying construction
Labor with the appropriate skill sets will be available	A labor shortage will delay construction

Impacts

The project to move the family's belongings into the home is dependent upon the timely completion of this project.

Change Control Process

The project sponsor must approve the following changes:

- Any change that delays the date of occupancy beyond 8/15
- Any change that alters the approved design
- Any change that increases the budget by 5% or more

The project manager will present these changes to the sponsor

Project Approach Document

The Jackson Home

January 15, xxxx

Project Approach Document
January 15, XXXX

The quality of the home that is constructed as a result of this project is of utmost importance. For this reason, selection of the builder will be the first item to be addressed.

The selection process will include:

♦ Evaluations of the number of homes built in the area

♦ The builder's local market share

♦ The number and type of repairs needed in the first year of occupancy

♦ The percentage of homes that are completed on schedule

♦ Visits to completed homes and homes under construction

♦ Average construction costs per square foot

The builder will be selected after this information has been gathered and evaluated.

The sponsors will develop the initial project requirements. The team will meet with the selected builder to review and enhance these requirements. Available building sites will then be evaluated against these requirements and the selection made. The evaluation process will include visits to at least five potential building sites.

The design requirements will be submitted to an architect recommended by the builder. Drafts of the design will be reviewed with the project team and appropriate adjustments made.

Construction will begin after the sponsors have approved the design. The builder will provide weekly written status reports to the project team. Issues will be addressed in bi-weekly project status meetings.

Project Plan

#	Task Name	Duration	Start	Finish	Predecessor	Resource
1	**Select Builder**	**22days**	**1/3**	**2/1**		
2	Interview Builders	10days	1/3	1/14		Sponsor
3	Make Builder Selection	12days	1/17	2/1	2	Sponsor
4	Define Requirements	20days	2/2	2/29		
5	Meet with stakeholders	10days	2/2	2/15	3	Builder
6	Assemble requirements	5days	2/16	2/22	5	Builder
7	Review with stakeholders	5days	2/23	2/29	6	Builder
8	**Select Building Location**	**11days**	**3/1**	**3/15**		
9	Review Options	2days	3/1	3/2	7	Sponsor
10	Complete Site Visits	5days	3/3	3/9	9	Sponsor
11	Make Site Selection	4days	3/10	3/15	10	Sponsor
12	**Complete Design**	**93days**	**3/1**	**7/7**		
13	Forward Requirements to Architect	1day	3/1	3/1	7	Builder
14	Forward location specs to Architect	1day	3/16	3/16	11	Builder
15	Complete Design	15days	3/17	4/6	14	Architect
16	Review design with stakeholders	2days	4/7	4/10	15	Architect
17	Approve Design	5days	4/11	4/17	16	Sponsor
18	Final Trim Specs Due	1day	5/29	5/29		Sponsor
19	Final Lighting specs Due	1day	6/5	6/5		Sponsor
20	Final Paint Specs Due	1day	6/30	6/30		Sponsor
21	Final Flooring Specs Due	1day	7/3	7/3		Sponsor
22	Final Cabinet Specs Due	1day	7/3	7/3		Sponsor
23	Final Fixture Specs Due	1day	7/7	7/7		Sponsor
24	**Construction**	**84days**	**4/18**	**8/11**		
25	Procure materials	10days	7/4	7/17	21	Builder
26	Secure Permits	5days	4/18	4/24	17	Builder
27	Assign labor	5days	4/18	4/24	17	Builder
28	Excavate Site	10days	4/25	5/8	27,26	Excavator
29	Pour Foundation & Driveway	6days	5/9	5/16	28	ConcreteCont
30	Build Frame	30days	5/17	6/27	29	Carpenter
31	Complete Roofing	4days	6/28	7/3	30 & 18	Roofer
32	Complete Exterior Sheeting	5days	6/28	7/4	30 & 18	Carpenter
33	Install Windows and Exterior Doors	3days	6/28	6/30	30 & 18	Carpenter
34	Complete Masonry	12days	7/5	7/20	32 & 18	Mason
35	Complete Electrical Installation	6days	7/5	7/12	31,32,33 & 39	Electrician
36	Complete Plumbing	6days	7/5	7/12	31 & 32	Plumber
37	Complete Heating/AC Installation	6days	7/10	7/17	23	Heating/AC
38	Complete Drywalling	7days	7/21	7/31	35,37,36 & 34	Drywaller
39	Install Cabinets	4days	8/1	8/4	38 & 22	Carpetner
40	Install Fixtures	4days	8/7	8/10	39 & 23	Plumber
41	Complete Painting	3days	8/1	8/3	38 & 20	Painter
42	Install Floor Coverings	2days	8/4	8/7	41 & 21	Floor Covering
43	Inspection	1day	8/11	8/11	40 & 42	
44	Review	1day	8/14	8/14		
45	Meet with Sponsor	1day	8/14	8/14	43	Builder
46	**Implement**	**1day**	**8/15**	**8/15**		
47	Take Occupancy	1day	8/15	8/15	45	Sponsor

Requirements Document
The Jackson Home
March 1, xxxx

Requirements Document

#	Area	Item	Requirement	Notes
1	Air Conditioning	Type	Central Air-conditioning shall be used	
2	Basement	Size	The structure shall have a full basement	
3	Basement	Facilities	The basement shall be "roughed" for a full bath	
4	Bathrooms	Number	The structure shall contain 2 full baths and one half-bath	
5	Bathrooms	Location	There shall be one full bath adjacent to the master bedroom, one full bath accessible from an upstairs hall and one half bath on the main level.	
6	Bathrooms	Fixtures	The master bath shall have separate tub and shower.	
7	Bathrooms	Fixtures	The full baths shall both have two sinks in a single countertop.	
8	Bathrooms	Fixtures	Specifics of brands and models shall be identified at least 30 days prior to installation	
9	Bathrooms	Flooring	The flooring of all bathrooms shall be tile. The specific design of the tile shall be decided at least 30 days prior to installation.	
10	Bathrooms	Size	The master bath shall not have a single dimension of less than 8 feet and a total area of not less than 80 sq ft.	
11	Bathrooms	Size	The hall bath shall not have a single dimension of less than 7 feet and a total area of not less than 70 sq ft.	
12	Bathrooms	Size	The half-bath shall not have a single dimension of less than 4 feet and a total area of not less than 30 sq ft	
13	Bedrooms	Size	No bedroom shall have a single dimension of less than 13 feet	
14	Bedrooms	Size	No bedroom shall have a total area of less than 150 sq. ft.	
15	Bedrooms	Size	The master bedroom shall not have a single dimension of less than 16 feet	
16	Bedrooms	Size	The area of the master bedroom shall not be less than 300 sq. ft.	
17	Bedrooms	Number	There shall be no fewer than 4 bedrooms	
18	Bedrooms	Location	All bedrooms shall be on the upper level	
19	Bedrooms	Windows	Every Bedroom shall have at least one window.	
20	Bedrooms	Ceiling Fans	Ceiling fans shall be installed in all bedrooms.	
21	Bedrooms	Ceiling Fans	Ceiling fans shall be selected at least 30 days prior to installation.	
22	Ceilings	Main Floor	The main floor ceilings shall be 9 feet from the floor	
23	Ceilings	Upper Floor	The upper floor ceilings shall be 8 feet from the floor	
24	Ceilings	Basement	The basement ceiling shall be no less than 8 feet from the floor.	
25	Ceilings	Garage	The garage ceiling shall be no less than 10 feet from the floor.	

26	Dining Room	Size	The dining room shall have no single dimension of less than 15 feet and a total area of no less than 180 square feet.
27	Dining Room	Location	The dining room shall be accessible directly from the kitchen
28	Electrical		The home shall be wired in compliance with all local regulations
29	Entry	Size	The front entry shall have no single dimension of less than 8 feet and a total area of not less than 64 sq ft
30	Entry	Flooring	The flooring of the front entry shall be oak
31	Exterior	Surface	The home shall have a brick front with board siding elsewhere
32	Exterior	Chimneys	The exterior surface of all chimneys will be brick, matching the front of the home
33	Floors	Type	Floors shall be carpeted unless otherwise indicated
34	Garage	Size	The garage shall be no less than 24 feet wide and 20 feet deep
35	Garage	Location	The garage shall be attached to the home.
36	Garage	Entry	The garage shall be entered form the side of the home (garage door not facing the street)
37	Garage Door	Size	The door shall be no less than 18 feet wide.
38	Garage Door	Style	The garage door shall be an overhead door. The specific appearance of the door shall be decided at least 30 days prior to installation.
39	Great Room	Size	The great room shall have no single dimension of less then 16 feet and a total area of no less than 380 sq ft
40	Great Room	Fireplace	The great room shall include a wood-burning fireplace
41	Heating	Type	Gas Heating shall be used
42	Insulation	Attic	Attic insulation shall be no less than R-30
43	Insulation	Exterior Walls	Exterior wall insulation shall be no less than R-15
44	Kitchen	Location	The kitchen shall be located with a view of the great room and of the back yard
45	Kitchen	Size	The kitchen shall have no single dimension of less then 15 feet and a total area of no less than 300 sq ft
46	Kitchen	Flooring	The flooring of the kitchen shall be tile. The specific design shall be identified at least 30 days prior to installation
47	Kitchen	Appliances	The kitchen shall contain a conventional stove, microwave, refrigerator, dishwasher and disposal. The specific designs of the appliances shall be decided at least 30 days prior to installation.
48	Kitchen	Counter top	The kitchen shall contain at least 60 square feet of counter space
49	Kitchen	Counter top	The specific design of the counter top surface shall be decided at least 30 days prior to installation.
50	Laundry	Size	The laundry room shall have no single dimension of less then 8 feet and a total area of no less than 80 sq ft

51	Laundry	Flooring	The flooring of the laundry room shall be tile
52	Laundry	Lighting	The laundry room shall have overhead lighting and at least one wall switch.
53	Light Fixtures	Location	All bedrooms shall have overhead lighting with at least one wall switch.
54	Light Fixtures	Type	Specifics of brands and models shall be identified at least 30 days prior to installation
55	Living Room		The structure shall not contain a living room
56	Lot	Size	The lot shall be no less than 1/2 acre
57	Lot	Location	The lot shall be no more than 1/4 mile from the local elementary school
58	Lot	Topography	The lot shall have a grade of no more than 2%.
59	Structure	Size	The structure shall be a two-story home with no less than 3000 square feet of living space
60	Water heater	Type	A gas water heater shall be used
61	Water heater	Capacity	A single water heater of at least 50 gallons
62	Windows	Type	Double-hung windows will be used where ever possible
63	Windows	Insulation	Triple-pane thermal windows shall be used

Design Document

The Jackson Home
April 15, xxxx

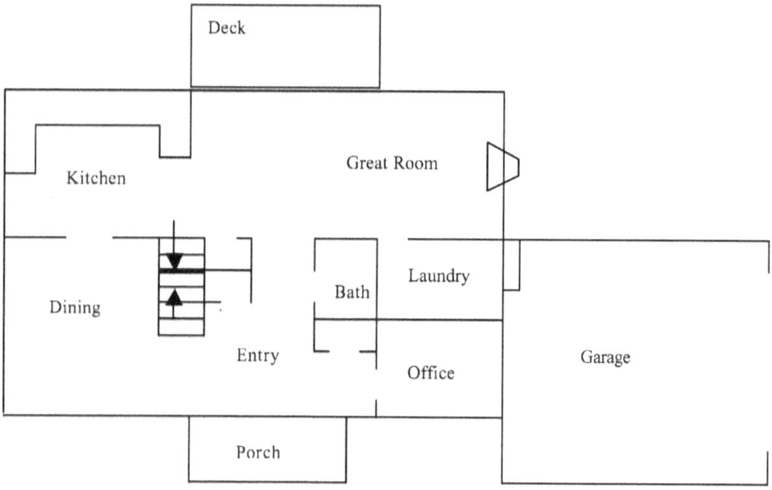
Deck
Kitchen
Great Room
Dining
Bath
Laundry
Entry
Office
Garage
Porch

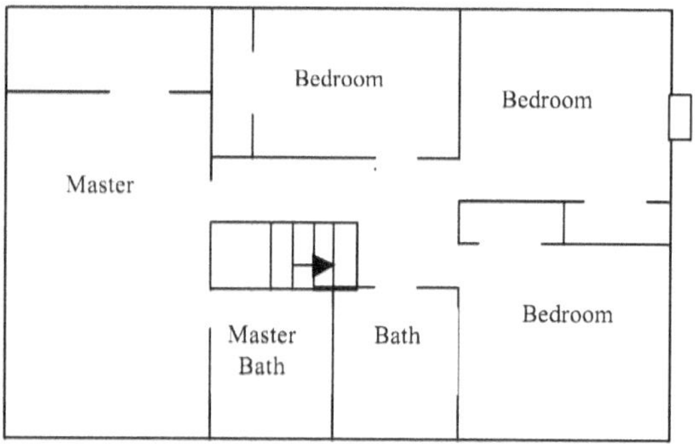
Bedroom
Bedroom
Master
Bedroom
Master
Bath
Bath

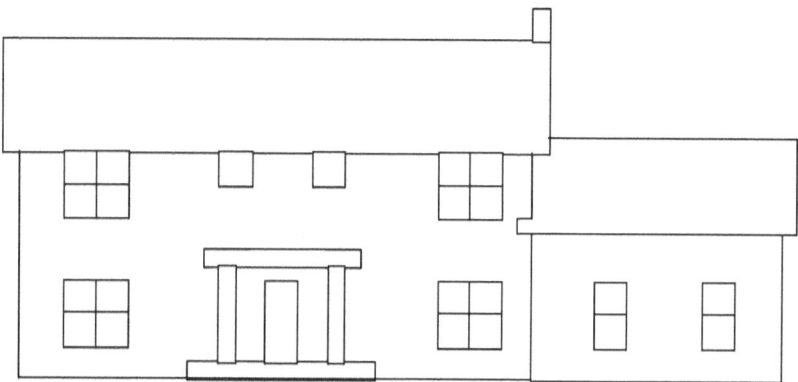

#	Area	Item	Requirement	Design Feature
1	Air Conditioning	Type	Central Air Conditioning shall be used	Central Air Conditioning shall be used
2	Basement	Size	The structure shall have a full basement	The structure shall have a full basement
3	Basement	Facilities	The basement shall be "roughed" for a full bath	The design features a "roughed" full bath in the basement
4	Bathrooms	Number	The structure shall contain 2 full baths and one half-bath	The structure contains 2 full baths and one half-bath
5	Bathrooms	Location	There shall be one full bath adjacent to the master bedroom, one full bath accessible from an upstairs hall and one half bath on the main level.	The design features one full bath adjacent to the master bedroom, one full bath accessible from an upstairs hall and one half bath on the main level.
6	Bathrooms	Fixtures	The master bath shall have separate tub and shower.	The master bath features separate tub and shower.
7	Bathrooms	Fixtures	The full baths shall both have two sinks in a single countertop.	The full baths each have two sinks in a single countertop.
8	Bathrooms	Fixtures	Specifics of brands and models shall be identified at least 30 days prior to installation	
9	Bathrooms	Flooring	The flooring of all bathrooms shall be tile. The specific design of the tile shall be decided at least 30 days prior to installation.	The design accommodates any type of flooring
10	Bathrooms	Size	The master bath shall not have a single dimension of less than 8 feet and a total area of not less than 80 sq ft.	The master bath measures 8 x 10 ft (80 sq ft)
11	Bathrooms	Size	The hall bath shall not have a single dimension of less than 7 feet and a total area of not less than 70 sq ft.	The hall bath measures 8 x 10 ft (80 sq ft)
12	Bathrooms	Size	The half-bath shall not have a single dimension of less than 4 feet and a total area of not less than 30 sq ft	The half bath measures 7 x 5 ft (35 sq ft)
13	Bedrooms	Size	No bedroom shall have a single dimension of less than 13 feet	The bedrooms measure 14 x 16, 16 x 16, 16 x 16 and 16 x 20.
14	Bedrooms	Size	No bedroom shall have a total area of less than 150 sq. ft.	The bedroom areas are 224, 256, 256 and 320 sq ft.
15	Bedrooms	Size	The master bedroom shall not have a single dimension of less than 16 feet	The master bedroom measures 16 x 20 feet
16	Bedrooms	Size	The area of the master bedroom shall not be less than 300 sq. ft.	The area of the master bedroom is 320 sq. ft.

17	Bedrooms	Number	There shall be no fewer than 4 bedrooms	There design features 4 bedrooms
18	Bedrooms	Location	All bedrooms shall be on the upper level	All bedrooms are on the upper level
19	Bedrooms	Windows	Every Bedroom shall have at least one window.	Every Bedroom has at least one window.
20	Bedrooms	Ceiling Fans	Ceiling fans shall be installed in all bedrooms.	All bedrooms are wired for ceiling fans
21	Bedrooms	Ceiling Fans	Ceiling fans shall be selected at least 30 days prior to installation.	
22	Ceilings	Main Floor	The main floor ceilings shall be 9 feet from the floor	The main floor ceilings are 9 feet from the floor
23	Ceilings	Upper Floor	The upper floor ceilings shall be 8 feet from the floor	The upper floor ceilings are 8 feet from the floor
24	Ceilings	Basement	The basement ceiling shall be no less than 8 feet from the floor.	The basement ceiling is 9 feet from the floor.
25	Ceilings	Garage	The garage ceiling shall be no less than 10 feet from the floor.	The garage ceiling shall be is 11feet from the floor.
26	Dining Room	Size	The dining room shall have no single dimension of less than 15 feet and a total area of no less than 180 square feet.	The dining room measures 16 x 18 feet (288 sq ft)
27	Dining Room	Location	The dining room shall be accessible directly from the kitchen	The dining room is accessible directly from the kitchen
28	Electrical		The home shall be wired in compliance with all local regulations	The wiring is in compliance with all local regulations
29	Entry	Size	The front entry shall have no single dimension of less than 8 feet and a total area of not less than 64 sq ft	The front entry measures 12 x 12 ft (144 sq ft)
30	Entry	Flooring	The flooring of the front entry shall be oak	The flooring of the front entry is oak planks
31	Exterior	Surface	The home shall have a brick front with board siding elsewhere	The design features a brick front with board siding elsewhere
32	Exterior	Chimneys	The exterior surface of all chimneys will be brick, matching the front of the home	The exterior surface of all chimneys is brick
33	Floors	Type	Floors shall be carpeted unless otherwise indicated	Floors are carpeted unless otherwise indicated
34	Garage	Size	The garage shall be no less than 24 feet wide and 20 feet deep	The garage measures 24 x 21 feet
35	Garage	Location	The garage shall be attached to the home.	The home features an attached garage.

36	Garage	Entry	The garage shall be entered form the side of the home (garage door not facing the street)	The garage entrance is on the side of the home (garage door not facing the street). Features of the lot required that the width of the driveway be reduced from the standard 15' to 12'.
37	Garage Door	Size	The door shall be no less than 18 feet wide.	The garage door shall is 18 feet wide.
38	Garage Door	Style	The garage door shall be a single overhead door. The specific appearance of the door shall be decided at least 30 days prior to installation.	The garage door is a single overhead door.
39	Great Room	Size	The great room shall have no single dimension of less then 16 feet and a total area of no less than 380 sq ft	The great room measures 16x24 feet (384 sq ft)
40	Great Room	Fireplace	The great room shall include a wood-burning fireplace	The great room features a wood-burning fireplace
41	Heting	Type	Gas Heating shall be used	Gas Heating shall be used
42	Insulation	Attic	Attic insulation shall be no less than R-30	Attic insulation is rated at R-35
43	Insulation	Exterior Walls	Exterior wall insulation shall be no less than R-15	Exterior wall insulation is rated R-15
44	Kitchen	Location	The kitchen shall be located with a view of the great room and of the back yard	The kitchen is located with a view of the great room and of the back yard
45	Kitchen	Size	The kitchen shall have no single dimension of less then 15 feet and a total area of no less than 300 sq ft	The kitchen measures 16 x 20 feet (320 sq ft)
46	Kitchen	Flooring	The flooring of the kitchen shall be tile. The specific design shall be identified at least 30 days prior to installation	The flooring of the kitchen is tile. The specific design shall be identified at least 30 days prior to installation
47	Kitchen	Appliances	The kitchen shall contain a conventional stove, microwave, refrigerator, dishwasher and disposal. The specific designs of the appliances shall be decided at least 30 days prior to installation.	The kitchen contains a conventional stove, microwave, refrigerator, dishwasher and disposal.
48	Kitchen	Counter top	The kitchen shall contain at least 60 square feet of counter space	The kitchen contains 65 square feet of counter space
49	Kitchen	Counter top	The specific design of the counter top surface shall be decided at least 30 days prior to installation.	
50	Laundry	Size	The laundry room shall have no single dimension of less then 8 feet and a total area of no less than 80 sq ft	The laundry room measures 12 x 13 feet (168 sq ft)
51	Laundry	Flooring	The flooring of the laundry room shall be tile	The flooring of the laundry room is tile
52	Laundry	Lighting	The laundry room shall have overhead lighting and at least one wall switch.	The laundry room has overhead lighting and two wall switches

53	Light Fixtures	Location	All bedrooms shall have overhead lighting with at least one wall switch.	All bedrooms have overhead lighting with at least one wall switch
54	Light Fixtures	Type	Specifics of brands and models shall be identified at least 30 days prior to installation	
55	Living Room		The structure shall not contain a living room	The structure does not contain a living room
56	Lot	Size	The lot shall be no less than 1/2 acre	The lot area is 1/2 acre
57	Lot	Location	The lot shall be no more than 1/4 mile from the local elementary school	The lot is 1/3 mile from the local elementary school
58	Lot	Topography	The lot shall have a grade of no more than 2%.	The lot is level (no grade).
59	Structure	Size	The structure shall be a two-story home with no less than 3000 square feet of living space	The structure is a two-story home with 3100 square feet of living space
60	Water heater	Type	A gas water heater shall be used	A single, gas, 50-gallon water heater will be used
61	Water heater	Capacity	A single water heater of at least 50 gallons	A single, gas, 50-gallon water heater will be used
62	Windows	Type	Double-hung windows will be used where ever possible	Double-hung windows are used throughout the home
63	Windows	Insulation	Triple-pane thermal windows will be used	Triple-pane thermal windows will be used throughout the home

Project Status Reports

Status Report-	Project Name: *The Jackson Home* Project Sponsor: *The Jackson Family* Project Manager: *Johnny Builder*	*March 15, XXXX*

Goal Statement*: To design and construct a residence for the Jackson family*

This Week's Goals	% Complete	Next Week's Goals	Issues
Selection of Building Site	90	Forward Location Specs to Architect	Weather has delayed site inspections

Comments- Heavy rains have delayed site inspections. Conditions are expected to improve and the site will be selected before 3/19. The architect has been able to begin design work as all of the sites have similar topography. The project time line should not be impacted.

Project Milestones

Milestone	Original Target Date	Revised Target Date	Status
Define Requirements	3/1/xx	3/1/xx	Complete
Select Location	3/15/xx	3/19/xx	Green
Complete Design	4/1/xx	4/1/xx	Green
Begin Construction	4/25/xx	4/25/xx	Green

Status Report-	Project Name: *The Jackson Home* Project Sponsor: *The Jackson Family* Project Manager: *Johnny Builder*	*May 1, XXXX*

Goal Statement*: To design and construct a residence for the Jackson family*

This Week's Goals	% Complete	Next Week's Goals	Issues
Complete labor Assignment	100	Complete Excavation	Road improvements are
Secure Permits	100		behind schedule, will not impact timeline if completed by 5/17

Comments- Resources assigned to road improvements have been called to other projects. There is lag time on the improvements to 5/17. Improvements should be completed prior to that date.

Project Milestones

Milestone	Original Target Date	Revised Target Date	Status
Complete Design	4/1/xx	4/1/xx	Complete
Begin Construction	4/25/xx	4/25/xx	Green
Foundation Complete	5/16/xx	5/16/xx	Green
Frame Complete	6/27/xx	6/27/xx	Green

The Jackson Home
Meeting Summary
March 23, xxxx

Opening Remarks

The project is progressing on schedule. The selected site is 1/3 mile from the local school, which violates the success criteria of a site within 1/4 mile of the school. The project sponsor has approved this variance.

Review of Project Plan

The progress of the project in relation to the project plan is very good. The overall status is "Green". The requirements are complete and the design team is on schedule to deliver the design for approval on 4/7.

Review of Issues List

No issues are due this week.

A new issue was identified involving the driveway. The requirements state that the structure have a side-entry garage. The selected lot does not provide sufficient area for a standard driveway in that configuration. The chief architect was assigned to present options to the project team at the March 30 meeting.

Other News/Discussion/Questions

There was discussion of the possibility of adding larger deck to the back of the house in the future. This impacts the placement of the air conditioning unit. It was decided that the air conditioning unit should be placed on the side of the house (rather than the back) to allow for possible future expansion of the deck.

Notes on future meetings

The next meeting will be at 1:00 PM on March 30 via conference call.

Issues Log

Issue Count: 4

The Jackson Home

Date: 6/15/xx

#	Description	Date Open	Status	Priority	Assigned To	Due Date	Deliverables/ Milestones Impacted	Date Closed	Resolution/Comments
4	Other projects diverting resources. Framing unable to make up lost time caused by heavy rains in May	6/15/xx	Open	High	Builder	6/22	Build Frame		Exploring Options
				Closed Issues					
1	Site will not allow side entry drive with 15' driveway	3/23/xx	Closed	High	Architect	3/30/xx	Finalize Design	4/1/xx	The width of the driveway will be reduced to 12'
2	Rain is slowing excavation	4/27/xx	Closed	High	Builder	4/30/xx	Excavate Site	4/30/xx	Excavation team will work overtime until caught up. Delivery date of excavation delayed 1 day, will not significantly impact overall budget
3	Rain delays foundation	5/10/xx	Closed	High	Builder	5/12/xx	Pour Foundation	5/12/xx	4 consecutive days of heavy rain delayed the pouring of the foundation. When weather cleared, the site was unsuitable for concrete work for and additional 2 days. Water was pumped from the site, foundation poured 6 days behind schedule. Planning to make up time with overtime in framing.

Project Signoff

The Jackson Home

August 31, XXXX

Goals

To design and construct a residence for the Jackson family

Completion Criteria

- The residence is ready for occupancy in compliance with all applicable laws and regulations
  Complete
- Construction is complete as specified in the design
  Complete
- Landscaping is completed as specified in the design
  Complete
- All remnants of construction (tools, scrap materials, signs, etc) have been removed from the property
  Complete

Success Criteria

Measure	Previous Environment	Target Environment	Result
Number of Bedrooms	3	4	4
Distance to School	2 Miles	1/4 Mile	1/3 Mile
Size of Garage	1 Car	2 Car	2 Car
Size of lot	1/4 acre	1/2 Acre	1/2 Acre

The "Distance to School" criteria was not met due to the selection of the building site. The project team participated in the selection and was aware of the impacts of the selection.

Outstanding Issues and Recommendations

There are no outstanding issues

Lessons Learned

The original timeline was very dependent upon good weather. The project experienced numerous, short delays as a result of poor weather. Efforts will be made in the future to accommodate potential weather problems in the timeline.

Ongoing Maintenance

The structure will be inspected by the builder monthly for the first 12 months and necessary repairs scheduled.

Approvals	
Project Sponsor:	Date:
Program Manager:	Date:
Project Manager:	Date:
	Date:
Comments	

Glossary of Terms

- **Approach** The methodology to be used by the project team
- **Approach Document** A document that describes the approach
- **Approval** Documented agreement with the contents of a document.
- **Assumption** A condition on which an aspect of the project depends
- **Budget** A schedule of the funds allotted to a project and when they are to be spent
- **Build** The phase of the project that creates the target environment
- **Capital Expenditures** Funds used to purchase depreciable assets
- **Change Control Process** A procedure outlined in the charter document that describes the process to revise items contained in the charter
- **Charter** A document that defines the goals, methodology, benefits and deliverables of a project
- **Clients** The group that receives the benefit of the project effort, also, the group that is supplying the funding for the project
- **Closed Issues** Issues that have been resolved.
- **Closure** The end of an effort. Closure can apply to tasks, issues or deliverables
- **Company** The business entity that has is responsible for the project
- **Completion Criteria** The specific deliverables that denote the end of the project. These are documented in the project charter
- **Concept** The vision of what the project will accomplish
- **Constraints** Limits or bounds that are placed on a project
- **Contract Labor** Temporary employees

- **Customers** The group that receives the benefit of the project effort, also, the group that is supplying the funding for the project
- **Deliverables** Specific, tangible items to be created
- **Dependency** A relationship between two or more tasks in a project plan where one task cannot be completed until another task is completed.
- **Depreciation** A periodic reduction in the value of an asset
- **Design** The planned outcome of the project. A diagram of the deliverable.
- **Design Document** A document that describes the design
- **Detail Plan** A form of project plan that describes all of the tasks involved
- **Detail Requirements** A document that describes the specific requirements of a project in exact terms
- **Distribution** The individuals that receive a document
- **Duration** The amount of time required to complete the task
- **Evidence of Completion** Tangible proof that a task or deliverable has been completed
- **Executive Summary** A brief description of the project
- **Expenses** Funds used for project costs other than the purchase of capital items
- **External Resources** Individuals that contribute to the project that are not regular employees of the company
- **Facilitate** The act of guiding a group to a conclusion
- **Facilitated Session** A meeting led by a facilitator
- **Facilitator** An individual that leads a group to a conclusion
- **Fixed Documents** Documents that do not change after approval
- **Goal Statement** A phrase that describes the objective of the project
- **High Level Plan** A form of project plan that summarizes like tasks

- **High Level Requirements** Project requirements that summarizes like items
- **Internal Resources** Individuals that contribute to the project that are regular employees of the company
- **Impacts** The affect that the project will have on other areas of the company
- **Implement** The migration from the current environment to the target environment
- **Issue** An unexpected event or circumstance that impacts the project
- **Issue List** A document that lists and describes issues
- **Issue Resolution** The steps necessary to eliminate or reduce the affect of the issue
- **First Meeting** The initial gathering of the projects team.
- **Living Documents** Documents that are revised on a routine basis
- **Managing Expectations** Ensuring that there is a clear understanding of what the project will and will not deliver.
- **Meeting Summaries** A document that describes the highlights of a meeting
- **Milestones** Key points in the project plan that can be used to measure progress
- **Open Issues** Issues that have not been resolved
- **Organization** The business entity that has is responsible for the project
- **Predecessor** A task on which another task is dependent
- **Program** A group of projects that are connected to each other through related goals or shared resources
- **Program Manager** The individual responsible for the coordination of a program
- **Project** An initiative within an organization designed to accomplish a specific goal with a clear starting point and ending point

- **Project Coordinator** An individual that assists the project manager in documenting, communicating and coordinating the project efforts
- **Project Justification** A measurement of the costs and benefits of a project
- **Project Manager** The individual accountable for the successful completion of all project deliverables.
- **Project Plan** A document that lists the items that must be completed to deliver the project objectives and the relationship between these items
- **Reporting** The process of distributing information about the project
- **Requirements** The stipulations of the target environment as described by the stakeholders
- **Resources** Individuals that are assigned to a project or task
- **Review** An informal examination of a document
- **Risk** An item or issue that potentially threatens the team's ability to deliver the project objectives
- **Scope** The boundaries of the project effort
- **Session** A gathering of the resources assigned to a deliverable
- **Signoff** Documented approval of a deliverable
- **Sponsor** An executive that is the primary supporter of the project
- **Stakeholder** Individuals and areas that are impacted by the project
- **Status** The condition of the project at a specific time
- **Status Meeting** A periodic meeting to discuss the condition of the project
- **Status Report** A document that describes the condition of the project at a specific time
- **Success Criteria** The specific results that are expected as a result of the project
- **Summary Tasks** A high-level task that consists of several smaller tasks

- **Task** A specific item to be completed
- **Team Member** An individual that serves on a project team
- **Templates** A standard document with pre-set headings and text that is used as a guide for creating project documents
- **Working Meeting** A gathering to accomplish a specific objective